Language and P
Gaeltacht and Sc
Review and Impact

John M. Kirk and Dónall P. Ó Baoill

Cló Ollscoil na Banríona
2011

First published in 2011
Cló Ollscoil na Banríona
Queen's University Belfast
Belfast, BT7 1NN

© 2011 Cló Ollscoil na Banríona and the authors

The text of this pamphlet is also published in *Strategies for Minority Languages: Northern Ireland, the Republic of Ireland, and Scotland*, eds. John M. Kirk and Dónall P. Ó Baoill (Belfast: Cló Ollscoil na Banríona, 2011) pp. 267–299.

The publication of this pamphlet has been made possible through the financial support of Foras na Gaeilge and Colmcille.

British Library Cataloguing-in-Publication Data
A catalogue record for this book is available from the British Library.

ISBN 978 0 85389 987 7

Typeset by Nigel Craig and John Kirk in Granjon
Cover map and design by Colin Young
Printing by Northside Graphics Ltd., Belfast

Ten Years of Language and Politics: Impact and Whither Now?

John M. Kirk and Dónall P. Ó Baoill[*]

This paper reviews the ten years of Language and Politics symposia on the Gaeltacht and Scotstacht which have been held at Queen's University Belfast from 2000–2010. It addresses the impact which the symposia have made and considers their possible futures.

Background

The inspiration for the symposia came directly from the *Belfast / Good Friday Agreement* of 1998 which propelled language centre-stage. But they also came about because, following Dónall Ó Baoill's appointment as Professor of Irish at Queen's in July 1998, we were eager to work together and cross the boundaries between our subjects in a genuinely inter-disciplinary way. Without either that ambition or the good rapport which we established, the symposia would not have happened.

The Agreement states:

> All participants recognize the importance of respect, understanding and tolerance in relation to linguistic diversity, including in Northern Ireland, the Irish language, Ulster-Scots and the languages of the various ethnic communities, all of which are part of the cultural wealth of the island of Ireland.

Whereas that statement was a dynamic declaration of recognition, it entailed of itself no further action. It was in the next paragraph, with reference to the aspirations of the *European Charter for Regional or Minority Languages*[1] that a commitment to action was stated:

> In the context of active consideration currently being given to the UK signing the Council of Europe Charter for Regional or Minority Languages, the British Government will in particular in relation to the Irish language, where appropriate and where people so desire it:
> - take resolute action to promote the language;
> - facilitate and encourage the use of the language in speech and writing in public and private life where there is appropriate demand;
> - seek to remove, where possible, restrictions which would discourage or work against the maintenance or development of the language;
> - make provision for liaising with the Irish language community, representing their views to public authorities and investigating complaints;
> - place a statutory duty on the Department of Education to encourage and facilitate Irish medium education in line with current provision for integrated education;

---

[*] We are most grateful to Gavin Falconer, Wilson McLeod, Colin Neilands and Dónall Ó Riagáin for comments on an earlier draft, and to all those who took part in the discussion on 21 September 2010 about the future of the project.

[1] '*The European Charter for Regional or Minority Languages* is a European treaty (CETS 148) adopted in 1992 under the auspices of the Council of Europe to protect and promote historical regional and minority languages in Europe. It is to be found at conventions.coe.int/Treaty/EN/Treaties/html/148.htm.

- explore urgently with the relevant British authorities, and in cooperation with the Irish broadcasting authorities, the scope for achieving more widespread availability of Teilifís na Gaeilge in Northern Ireland;
- seek more effective ways to encourage and provide financial support for Irish language film and television production in Northern Ireland; and
- encourage the parties to secure agreement that this commitment will be sustained by a new Assembly in a way which takes account of the desires and sensitivities of the community.

Although these wordings are directly taken over from the European Charter, the Charter had not, by 1998, been signed by the UK Government. No doubt under the pressure of the *Belfast Agreement, 1998,* the UK Government finally signed the Charter on 17 March 2000 and ratified it to take effect from 1 July 2001.

Languages which are official within regions or provinces or federal units within a State (e.g. Catalan in Spain) but which are not classified as official languages of the State may not benefit from the Charter. Nor may dialects of State languages (such as Hiberno-English or Scottish English). On the other hand, the Republic of Ireland has not signed the Charter on behalf of the Irish language as a minority language for it is designated as a 'national' language. Although France signed the Charter, it has not ratified it on behalf of its other languages because of its Constitution in favour of French as the sole language of State.

The Charter provides a large number of different actions which national governments can take to protect and promote historical regional and minority languages. There are two levels of protection – all signatories must apply the lower level of protection (as specified in Part II of the Charter) to qualifying languages. Signatories may further declare that a qualifying language or languages will benefit from the higher level of protection (Part III). Part III lists a range of actions from which states must agree to undertake at least 35.

The UK Government ratified the Charter with regard to Scottish Gaelic and Scots in Scotland; Welsh in Wales; and Irish and, doubtlessly following the *Belfast Agreement*, what was referred to as 'Ulster-Scots' in Northern Ireland, although for us it is a dialect of Scots (cf. Kirk 1998, 2004, 2011).[2]

The Charter is an international convention and thus has status under international law (Dónall Ó Riagáin, personal communication). By ratifying it to bring it into force, the UK Government and its devolved institutions were committing themselves to courses of action with regard to the languages named, to producing reports on those action every three years, and to receiving feedback on those reports by the Council of Europe's Committee of Experts.[3] These commitments, according to Ó Riagáin (2001), are 'real and substantive' and, with regard to Scots as well as Irish, 'necessitate a dramatic shift in public perception of linguistic diversity in Northern Ireland'.

The first group of commitments – known as Part II provisions – are of a general nature and set out the broad areas of principle that underpin the thrust of the Charter. The second group – set out in Part III – are specific and appear under the following headings: 'education', 'judicial proceedings', 'administration', 'media', 'culture', 'economic issues', and 'trans-frontier links'.

---

[2] In 2002, Cornish was added for England. In 2003, Manx Gaelic was also added to the UK instrument of ratification.

[3] These reports may be found at conventions.coe.int/treaty/Commun/ChercheSig.asp?NT=148and CM=1and DF=and CL=ENG.

Dónall Ó Riagáin, one of the European Charter's authors, has expressed the view that, for minority languages and the development of a shared society in Northern Ireland, the Charter is 'a godsend'. 'It is not a concession to anyone. It is the application of European standards to all – standards of language rights, of human rights [...] an excellent basis for developing language policy.' (2001: 54)

As Tony Blair records in his autobiography *A Journey*, Ulster Scots (Ullans) became not only a very late inclusion in, but a deal-breaker for, the *Belfast / Good Friday Agreement* (2010: 173–4), so that the references to it alongside those to Irish could not be ignored.

Where Irish is referred to as 'the Irish language', there is no such designation around Ulster Scots, so how is its status to be interpreted? Is the 'language' designation of Irish to be conferred to Ulster Scots by co-textual association? Or is Ulster Scots a dialect, as linguists have been describing, or a variant of a sub-dialect as the *Scottish National Dictionary* has claimed? In *Statutory Instrument 1999 No. 859, The North/South Co-operation (Implementation Bodies) (Northern Ireland) Order 1999*, the status of Ulster Scots is defined as follows: 'Ullans [i.e. Ulster Scots] is to be understood as the variety of the Scots language traditionally found in parts of Northern Ireland and Donegal.' If the Scots found in Ulster is a dialect, variety or variant of Scots, why is the label 'Scots' not used? In due course, it emerged that activists were seeking to establish Scots in Ulster not so much as part of a dialect-based continuum with Scotland but as an apperceptionally-based but officially-backed counterbalance to Irish. As the *Belfast Agreement* had been so clearly influenced by the European Charter, and as the Charter does not deal with dialects (Article 1), Ulster Scots had to be classified as a language – a political rather than linguistic motivation.[4] Consequently, with the Charter's recognition of two 'minority or regional' languages in Northern Ireland, there emerged a further voice which cut across the provisions of the Charter and which called for equality between Irish and Ulster Scots in every respect, including funding, seeking to link the fate of each so that neither could benefit without the other.

And so, in the aftermath of the *Belfast / Good Friday Agreement*, it quickly became clear that political and linguistic opinion were not aligned. By 2000, we were struck by the need for a Forum for debate about both 'languages', where all sides and parties, linguists as well as politicians, implementers as well as practitioners, could participate. At the same time, it became clear that it would be pointless to discuss Irish and Ulster Scots in Northern Ireland without discussion of Irish and Ulster Scots in the Republic of Ireland (shared linguistic continua, separate jurisdictions), and Gaelic (separate language) and Scots (shared dialect) in Scotland (shared UK jurisdiction).

First Symposium

With these considerations in mind, **the first symposium** was organised for 12 August 2000, as a one-day event within *Dialect 2000*, a joint conference of the Forum for Research on the Languages of Scotland and Ulster (FRLSU), and the Irish Association for Applied Linguistics (IRAAL).[5] The primary theme for that day was 'discrimination', arising from the contention that provisions such as those in the European Charter were necessary because there was a feeling that speakers of those languages had been discriminated against. However, we widened the debate to include

---

[4] Ulster-Scots is included in the list of languages covered by the Charter. See languagecharter.eokik.hu/byLanguage.htm lists.

[5] The academic papers from *Dialect2000* are published as Kirk and Ó Baoill 2001a, with our long Introduction as Kirk and Ó Baoill 2001c.

gays,[6] speakers of immigrant languages,[7] and deaf speakers.[8] The then devolved Minister of Education, Seán Farren, gave an address.[9] The distinguished BBC NI broadcaster, Noel Thompson, chaired the entire proceedings, which were published in December 2000 as **Kirk and Ó Baoill 2000a**, with our long Introduction as Kirk and Ó Baoill 2000b.

Symposium Series

About that time, the then Arts and Humanities Board initiated a number of research centres, including one for Irish and Scottish Studies at the University of Aberdeen (RCISS), with Queen's University Belfast and Trinity College Dublin as junior partners. Because of its organisation of *Dialect 2000* with the Irish Association for Applied Linguistics (IRAAL), the FRLSU was invited by the centre's first director, Prof. Tom Devine, to contribute a series of symposia to the centre's work. The continuation of the languages and politics theme was an obvious choice, so that, in turn, on behalf of the FRLSU, we were invited to organise what became the next four symposia in 2001, 2002, 2003 and 2004. At the same time, for the purpose of wider dissemination, we became obliged to produce from each symposium an edited volume of proceedings (Kirk and Ó Baoill 2001, 2002, 2003, 2004.

Mindful that it was the European Charter which had inspired the provisions in the *Belfast / Good Friday Agreement*, we quickly decided that the programme for these seminars should not only deal with what we came to formulate as the Gaeltacht and Scotstacht,[10] covering Scotland and the Republic of Ireland as well as Northern Ireland, but also directly with the Charter's provisions and include as many non-academics and politicians as possible. At the same time, we decided to include presentations about other minority or regional languages, particularly in Europe, with which Irish and Ulster Scots might beneficially be compared.

The **second symposium**, in August 2001, thus addressed the issue of policy head-on. In addition, there were valuable comparisons with Frisian and with Norway and Switzerland. And papers or addresses were given by two MSPs (Mike Russell, MSP, who at the time was preparing a Private Member's Bill on Gaelic, and Irene McGugan, MSP, who had become the first chairperson of the Scottish Parliament's Cross-Party Group on the Scots Language), and by the Lord Laird of Artigarvan, by then the Chairman of the Board of the Ulster-Scots Agency. These papers are published as **Kirk and Ó Baoill 2001b**, with our long Introduction as Kirk and Ó Baoill 2001d. For a review, see Ó Riain [2002].

The **third symposium**, in September 2002, tackled the issue of Irish-medium and Gaelic-medium education. The question of Scots and education had a different orientation and was accompanied by a set of papers on issues of standardisation. Wider perspectives, particularly with regard to human rights, were raised in important keynote papers by the internationally renowned linguists Tove Skutnabb-Kangas and Robert Phillipson. And political papers were given by Irene McGugan, MSP, previously mentioned; the then Minister for Tourism, Culture and Leisure in the Scottish Executive; and the then Minister for Employment and Learning in the Northern Ireland Executive, Carmel Hanna, MLA. These papers are published as **Kirk and Ó**

---

[6] Mag Lochlainn 2000.
[7] Foley 2000, Watson 2000.
[8] McCullough 2000.
[9] Farren 2000.
[10] Our earliest use is in Kirk and Ó Baoill 2001b: 2.

Baoill 2002a, with our long Introduction as Kirk and Ó Baoill 2002c. For a review, see Bird 2004.

By then, we had covered four areas of the Charter's provision: 'status', 'discrimination', 'rights' and 'education'. The **fourth symposium**, in September 2003, tackled other areas of Part III provision: 'the media', 'cultural activities and facilities' and 'economic and social life'. We divided the papers into the following sections: 'broadcasting', 'the press', 'culture in the shape of the performing arts', and 'the economy'. International comparisons were made with Basque and Walloon. Éamon Ó Cuív, TD, Minister for Community, Rural and Gaeltacht Affairs, made an important after-dinner address on the Republic's views towards Irish in the light of the *Official Languages Act 2003*. One of the papers on language and the economy was given jointly by Esmond Birnie, MLA, and Steven King, then an adviser to David Trimble, First Minister.[11] These papers are published as **Kirk and Ó Baoill 2003a**, with our long Introduction as Kirk and Ó Baoill 2003b. For a review, see Simpson 2004 and Moriarty 2006.

The **fifth symposium**, in September 2005, concluded the survey of Part II provision by tackling the trans-frontier issue of Irish in the European Union, Irish by then having become an official language in the EU. It also tackled the impending Gaelic Bill in Scotland, the question of literary uses of Irish, Gaelic and Scots, and also the sociolinguistics of each language. Comparisons were also made with Maltese, which had provided the key to the recognition of Irish in the EU, and Kashubian. These papers are published as **Kirk and Ó Baoill 2005a**, with our long Introduction as Kirk and Ó Baoill 2005b.

During 2005, the AHRC RCISS became funded for a second period of five years from 2006–2010 (Phase II). This time, no doubt in reflection of the success of the first five symposia and accompanying publications, and the association of Queen's with the event, we became invited directly to organise a further five annual symposia and accompanying publications.

At the fourth symposium, in 2004, the session on language and economy proved so stimulating that we became urged to devote an entire symposium to the topic. This was the immediate choice of theme at the **sixth symposium** in September 2006. We had the good fortune that, for this purpose, François Grin devised a set of four paradigms which could link language with economic development and which each contributor addressed. As a result, we constructed a coherent set of position papers for Irish, Gaelic and Scots, some looking back to explain the present position, others looking forward to see how the matters could or should be developed. These papers were published as **Kirk and Ó Baoill 2009a**, with our Introduction as Kirk and Ó Baoill 2009b.

Following the sixth symposium, the *Northern Ireland (St Andrews Agreement) Act 2006* of December 2006 promised to bring forward heads of a Bill for a new *Irish Language Act* in Northern Ireland. Some Irish activists construed this as meaning that there would be an Irish Language Act. The British Government fulfilled the letter of the agreement by bringing forward heads for a Bill but the whole project was vetoed by the DUP. The Agreement also promised an Ulster-Scots Academy.

The **seventh symposium**, in November 2007, tackled the question of communities in which Irish, Gaelic and Scots were spoken, how they might be sustained, and what policies might ensure their sustainability. There was a central focus on the adequacy of

---

[11] Papers on many of the topics of this and the previous two symposia were also presented at a symposium on Language and Law in Northern Ireland, held at Stormont in February 2003, and published as Ó Riagáin 2003.

current arrangements and practices for minority languages in Ireland and Scotland, the importance of infrastructure, environment, society, employment, urban renewal, culture, the role of education, the vibrancy of the languages themselves, and whether minority language sustainability is a matter for a top-down or bottom-up approach. A further group of papers dealt with Scots, by applying similar questions, and a final set dealt with similar situations facing certain comparable minority languages elsewhere. These papers are published as **Kirk and Ó Baoill 2011a**, with our long Introduction as Kirk and Ó Baoill 2011c.

The **tenth symposium**, in September 2010, of which the present volume forms the edited proceedings, takes its cue from the publication of the draft *20-Year Strategy for the Irish Language*.[12] The symposium sought to consider what it means to be 'bilingual' in Ireland, what the role of policy and education to this end is supposed to be, and what wider concepts and experience need to be considered for implementing the 20-Year Strategy. Given the continuum of language but separation of jurisdiction, the symposium also focuses on the implications of the Strategy for Northern Ireland. A *Strategy for Indigenous or Regional Minority Languages* has long been promised by DCAL, but none so far has appeared. Finally, the symposium received a report on the first set of recommendations to the Scottish Government by the Ministerial Advisory Group on Scots. These papers are published as **Kirk and Ó Baoill 2011b**, with our long Introduction as Kirk and Ó Baoill 2011d.

By refering to our detailed Introductioons, we are mindful to oned reviewer's comment: '... anyone who finds it impossible to read [all these volumes] should, to make up the deficit, at least read the invaluable familiarising introductions provided in each volume by the editors ... .' (Macaulay 2002)

From these eight symposia, there have arisen eight core volumes of language and politics papers. Other papers by ourselves arising from the symposia are Kirk 2000a-b, 2004, 2005, 2008, 2010, 2011; and Ó Baoill 2001, 2002, 2004, 2005, 2006a-c, 2011a-b.

We should record that the **eighth symposium**, in November 2008, took on a different character and looked at the question of language and politics during the Age of Revolution which culminated in the Act of Union which took effect in 1801. Responses to the American Revolution and the French Revolution led to the creation of a huge body of poetry and songs in Irish, Gaelic, Scots, English and even Latin.[13] What emerges is that the responses to these historical events in each country in the different languages are varied and show different facets to radicalism in the face of loyalist oppression and backlash – hence the title of *United Islands?* From this symposium, and a sequel which was held in September 2009, two volumes of proceedings have been edited: **Kirk, Noble and Brown forthcoming, Kirk, Brown and Noble forthcoming.**

The **ninth symposium**, in October 2009, formed a thematic strand within the Sixth Irish-Scottish Academic Initiative Conference, entitled *Global Nations? Irish and Scottish Expansion since the 16th Century*, at the University of Aberdeen, where a range of language and politics papers as well as papers on language contact and borders were presented. As those papers were not published as a volume, the references are Connolly 2009, Dunbar 2009, Hickey, 2009, Kirk 2009, published as Kirk and Kallen 2011, Loester 2009, Millar 2009b, McCafferty 2009, McLeod 2009b, and Ó Riagáin 2009b.

Concurrent with these symposia during the first decade of the twenty-first century has been a number of key developments, which we now list:

---

[12] www.pobail.ie/ie/AnGhaeilge/.
[13] Of note here is the work of the Scottish radical, Rev. Alexander Geddes.

In the Republic of Ireland

For Irish
2002 *Official Languages (Equality) Bill, 2002.*
2003 *Official Languages Act 2003 / Acht na dTeangacha Oifigiúla 2003.*[14]
2003 Office of Irish Language Commissioner established.[15] Seán Ó Cuirreáin is appointed as first Commissioner.
2006 Rialtas na hÉireann / Government of Ireland, publication of *Ráiteas i Leith na Gaeilge 2006 / Statement on the Irish Language 2006.*[16]
2007, 1 January, Irish becomes an Official Language of the European Union.
2007 November. Publication of *Staidéar Teangeolaíoch ar Úsáid na Gaeilge sa Ghaeltacht / Comprehensive Linguistic Study of the Use of Irish in the Gaeltacht: Principal Findings and Recommendations.*[17]
2009 February. Publication of *20-Year Strategy for the Irish Language*, prepared for the Department of Community, Rural and Gaeltacht Affairs, by FIONTAR, Dublin City University.[18]
2010 April. Publication of *Dréacht-Straitéis 20-Bliain Don Ghaeilge 2010–2030 / Draft 20-Year Strategy for the Irish Language 2010–2030.*[19]
2010, December. Launch of the (final) *Straitéis 20-Bliain Don Ghaeilge 2010–2030 / 20-Year Strategy for the Irish Language 2010–2030.*[20]

In Northern Ireland

For Irish
1998 *Belfast Agreement* [the *Good Friday Agreement*].
1999 Establishment of the North/South Language Body (An Foras Teanga).
1999 Establishment of Foras na Gaeilge.
2001 Ratification of the *European Charter for Regional or Minority Languages (Chairt Eorpach um Theangacha Réigiúnacha nó Mionlaigh).*
2004 Announcement of Irish Language Broadcast Fund (Ciste Craoltóireachta na Gaeilge).
2008 Inter-departmental Charter Implementation Group.
2006 *Northern Ireland (St Andrews Agreement) Act*, interpreted by the Democratic Unionist Part as mandating a non-legislative strategy, and by the Irish-language community as mandating legislation.
A *Strategy for Indigenous or Regional Minority Languages* has long been announced by DCAL as forthcoming.

---

[14] The *Official Languages Act 2003 (Acht na dTeangacha Oifigiúla 2003)* sets out rules regarding use of the Irish language by public bodies, establishes the office of An Coimisinéir Teanga to monitor and enforce compliance by public bodies with the provisions of the *Official Languages Act* and makes provision for the designation of official Irish language versions of place-names and the removal of the official status of English place-names in the Gaeltacht. See Coisdelbha, in this volume.

[15] See www.coimisineir.ie/.

[16] For text, see www.pobail.ie/en/IrishLanguage/.

[17] A Research Report prepared for the for the Department of Community, Rural and Gaeltacht Affairs by Acadamh na hOllscolaíochta Gaeilge / National University of Ireland, Galway by Conchúr Ó Giollagáin and Seosamh Mac Donnacha, Fiona Ní Chualáin, Aoife Ní Shéaghdha and Mary O'Brien. For text, see www.pobail.ie/en/IrishLanguage/.

[18] This report was prepared by Peadar Ó Flatharta, Caoilfhionn Níc Pháidín, Colin Williams, François Grin, and Joseph Lo Bianco. For text, see www.pobail.ie/en/IrishLanguage/

[19] www.pobail.ie/en/IrishLanguage/Strategy/Strategy.pdf.

[20] www.pobail.ie/en/IrishLanguage/.

2011, May. Carál Ní Chuilín, new Minister for Culture, Arts and Leisure announces intention to revive the preparations for an *Irish Language Act*.

For Ulster Scots
1998 *Belfast Agreement* [the *Good Friday Agreement*].
1999 Establishment of the North/South Language Body (The Noarth/Sooth Leid Boadie).
1999 Establishment of the Ulster-Scots Agency (Tha Boord o Ulstèr-Scotch).
2001 Ratification of the *European Charter for Regional or Minority Languages (European Chairter fer Locail ir Minoritie Leids*).
2004 Announcement of Budget for an Ulster-Scots Academy.
2005–06 Ulster Scots Academy Implementation Group.
2006 Public Consultation on Ulster Scots Academy Implementation Group's proposals for an Ulster-Scots Academy.
2006 *Northern Ireland (St Andrews Agreement) Act*, which states: 'The Government firmly believes in the need to enhance and develop the Ulster-Scots language, heritage and culture and will support the incoming executive in taking this forward'.
2008 Inter-departmental Charter Implementation Group.
2009 Deloitte produce a Business Case for an Ulster-Scots Academy.
2011, March. Appointment of Chair and Members of Ministerial Advisory Group, Ulster-Scots Academy.
A *Strategy for Indigenous or Regional Minority Languages* has long been announced by DCAL as forthcoming.

In Scotland

For Gaelic[21]
1997 Publication of *Secure Status for Gaelic / Inbhe Thèarainte dhan Ghàidhlig* by Comunn na Gàidhlig.
1999 Presentation of *Draft Brief for a Gaelic Language Act / Dreach Iùil Airson Achd Gàidhlig* by Comunn na Gàidhlig.
2000 Publication of *Revitalising Gaelic: A National Asset* (The MacPherson Report)[22] which recommended that a Gaelic Development Agency should, *inter alia*, facilitate the process of achieving secure status for the language.
2002 Publication of *Cothrom Ùr don Ghàidhlig*, the Report by the Ministerial Advisory Group on Gaelic, chaired by Professor Donald Meek ('the Meek Report'), which set out further detail on the role and position of such a Development Agency and called for an Act.
2002 Private member's Bill on Gaelic (Michael Russell). This Bill aimed to require certain public bodies to publish, maintain and implement plans based on the principle that the Gaelic and English languages should be treated on a basis of equality as far as was appropriate in the circumstances and reasonably practicable.
2003, April, Establishment of Bòrd na Gàidhlig as an Executive Non-Departmental Public Body, which prepared the Gaelic Language Act.
2005 The *Gaelic Language (Scotland) Act 2005*. *Inter alia*, the Act established Bòrd na

---

[21] For a Gvernment narrative of these developments, see www.scotland.gov.uk/Topics/ArtsCultureSport/arts/gaelic/gaelic-english/17910/Gaelic-language-plan.
[22] For a critical appraisal by Alasdair MacCaluim and Wilson McLeod, see www.arts.ed.ac.uk/celtic/poileasaidh/ipcamacpherson2.pdf.

Gàidhlig as a national language planning body, requires the Bòrd to publish a National Gaelic Language Plan every five years and requires certain public authorities to prepare Gaelic Language Plans.[23]

2007 Bòrd na Gàidhlig publishes the first *National Gaelic Language Plan 2007–12*.

2008 Launch of the digital television service MG ALBA.

For Scots

2000 Scottish Executive *Creating our Future … Minding our Past: Scotland's National Cultural Strategy.*[24]

2004 Committee of Experts, First Monitoring Report on the European Charter.[25]

2007 Scottish Executive *A Strategy for the Scotland's Languages*. Draft version for consultation. Scottish Executive Education Department, Cultural Policy Division.[26]

2007 Committee of Experts, Second Monitoring Report on the European Charter.[27]

2008 Establishment of Scots Language Audit.

2009 February. Conference on the Scots Language, University of Stirling, at which the Audit Report was presented.

2009 Establishment of Ministerial Advisory Group on Scots, under the Chairmanship of J. Derrick McClure.

2010 Committee of Experts, Third Monitoring Report on the European Charter.[28]

2010. 30 November. Publication of Report of the Ministerial Advisory Group on Scots presented to the Scottish Government.[29]

2011. 18 March. Government Response to MAGOS Report published.

With regard to Irish and Gaelic, Scots and Ulster Scots, as these time lines indicate, in each of our jurisdictions, it has been a decade of activism and advocacy leading gradually but eventually to implementation, with differing political emphases in each jurisdiction. The pace of progress has inevitably been slow and uneven, with the reports by the ECRML Committee of Experts pointing to a considerable lack of progress particularly with regard to Scots and Ulster-Scots in need of addressing.

As these incremental milestones were ultimately reached, Language and Politics provided a forum for discussion and critical debate. Language and Politics was thus a child of its time, arising after the creation of the North/South Language Bodies, and also about the same time as Iomairt Cholm Cille, now simply known as Colmcille.[30] Many of those involved with the advocacy, advising, reporting and implementing have been the very people who have participated in the symposia. For them, critical reflection and appraisal which the symposia generated proved no only invaluable, there grew an

---

[23] For discussion of the Gaelic Plan for Glasgow, see Walsh and McLeod 2011.
[24] www.scotland.gov.uk/nationalculturalstrategy/docs/cult-00.asp.
[25] www.coe.int/t/dg4/education/minlang/Report/default_en.asp.
[26] www.scotland.gov.uk/Publications/2007/01/24130746/0. See also Scots Language Centre compilation of responses to *A Strategy for the Scotland's Languages*. Draft version. at www.scotslanguage.com/.
[27] see footnote 25.
[28] see footnote 25.
[29] For text of report, see www.scotland.gov.uk/Publications/2010/11/25121454/0; see also Robinson and Eagle, in this volume. For a report on the Group's work, see
[29] www.scotslanguage.com/articles/view/227830.
[30] According to its website, 'Colmcille is a partnership programme between Foras na Gaeilge and Bòrd na Gàidhlig, promoting the use of Irish Gaelic and Scottish Gaelic in Ireland and Scotland and between the two countries. Colmcille aims through its work to foster understanding of the diverse experience and culture of the Irish and Scottish Gaelic communities, and to encourage debate on common concerns in social, cultural and economic issues with a view to building self-confidence within the Gaelic language communities.' www.colmcille.net [accessed 7 April 2011].

inevitable and valuable symbiosis on both a North-South as well as East-West basis between their own groups and constituencies and the symposia, each influencing the other in incalculable ways, in an unstoppable cycle. The first decade of the new millennium has turned out to be a glotto-political journey for many, with the proceedings volumes documenting the way and providing documentation.

It has to be noted, however, with the exception of Colmcille, which cuts across all jurisdictions, no funding came directly to the symposia or their publications from any Scottish body, even although a sizeable component of our deliberations and papers was concerned with Gaelic and Scots. Academics and activists domiciled in Scotland regularly commented upon the fact that, to discuss the politics of Gaelic and Scots, they had to be invited to – and funded by – an event in Belfast.

Assessment

The success of these symposia was undoubtedly due to a cocktail of several ingredients. Firstly, within sociolinguistics, although many journals have carried relevant material for some time, such as the *International Journal for the Sociology of Language*, we have certainly helped with the development of 'Language and Politics' as a subject area or 'language policy and planning studies', to which some of the leading core textbooks now devote entire chapters,[31] and for which there are specialist textbooks,[32] and two journals.[33] However, our specific focus has been on the continua of the Gaeltacht, from the Butt of Lewis to the ring of Kerry, and what we came to call the Scotstacht, from Unst in Shetland to the Irish border counties Cavan, Donegal, and Monaghan.[34] Cutting across these continua are the political jurisdictions: the sovereign states of the Republic of Ireland and the United Kingdom of Great Britain and Northern Ireland and, within the latter, there are now devolved Executive/Government in Edinburgh and Belfast. In so doing, our orientation has been East/West as much as North/South, with Northern Ireland occupying a pivotal position between the two, being both British and Irish as well as neither, what Edna Longley has called a 'cultural corridor' or 'zone where Ireland and Britain permeate one another, with British and Irish identities open at either end' (1993: 340). For in each jurisdiction and within each devolved area, language policy has evolved separately, seemingly without co-ordination. Irish is treated very differently in the North from the South – and, whereas it is the same language, the *Official Languages Act 2003* and the 20-Year Strategy in the Republic do not apply to Northern Ireland, where an *Irish Language Act* was rejected by two of the five parties forming the 2007–11 power-sharing Administration through exercising a veto, despite a majority of consultation responses being in favour on two occasions. Arrangements for Scots in Edinburgh and Belfast have also pursued different directions, despite the UK Government's obligation to report by now three times on the European Charter, leading Kirk (2008) to conclude that the UK does not have a coherent language policy.

---

[31] e.g. Mesthrie et al. 2009; Meyerhoff 2006; Wardhaugh 2009.

[32] e.g. Kaplan and Baldauf 1997; Ricento 2005; Spolsky 2004, 2009.

[33] *Journal of Language Policy*, vol. 1–, 2002-, originally edited by Bernard Spolsky, published by Springer Verlag; *European Journal of Language Policy*, vol. 1–, 2009–, edited by Michael Kelly, published by Liverpool University Press. In *Language Policy*, of especial interest to the concerns our symposia are Walsh and McLeod 2007, a version of which was presented at the 2007 symposium, and Millar 2006.

[34] Within those continua, we were also interested in the various Travellers languages, particularly Gammon, or Irish Cant, a quite separate phenomenon from Scottish or Scots Cant. From a separate symposium, with supplementation, we edited a volume of papers **Kirk and Ó Baoill 2002b**, with our long Introduction as Kirk and Ó Baoill 2002d. The volume contains six candid descriptions and accounts of use and attitudes by Travellers themselves. The academic papers are interdisciplinary, dealing with linguistic phenomena as well as ethnic and cultural identity. For important reviews, see Bakker 2006, Matras 2006 and Salzmann 2007.

At each symposium, we have encouraged presentation in these languages, providing simultaneous translation facilities, quite a new experience for many.[35] We have edited and published in those languages.[36] Although our earlier Introductions were intended to summarise all articles and be of especial use for readers without Irish or Gaelic, we have provided full translations in later volumes.

The content of our symposia focussed centrally on language policy for the minority/regional languages in the three jurisdictions in question, taking our cue from the *European Charter for Regional or Minority Languages*. Through the symposia and their publications, we created a set of critical position papers on the Charter's domains for language use: education, law, administration and public authorities, the media, etc., as well as other areas. We identified connections and disconnections between languages, speakers, policies, and practices. We incorporated an international dimension which enabled valuable contextualisation and provided useful clarification and insights. We achieved a great mix of participation (see below). Through the exchange of academic insight and applied or vocational experience, we raised awareness of all aspects of the equation: especially declining linguistic diversity, the need and means for reversing such declines, and the sustainability, including economic sustainability, of languages and communities. There was a recurrent emphasis on education. For everyone who participated, we deepened the quality of discussion.

We were at all times conscious that parallel developments, some of them of an exciting and relevant nature, were happening in other European countries. We felt that we should exchange models of good practice, to see what we could learn from each other. Although the situation of Scots had already been compared with that of German-speaking Switzerland (Meier 1977) and Norway (e.g. McClure 1988, 1995, 1997, 2009; also Vikør 1993, 2001; Millar 2009) and of Frisian (Meier 1997, Görlach 1985), for each we invited fresh reviews (Fischer, 2001, McCafferty 2001, Görlach 2001). Likewise, Celtic connections have long been made with Basque, Galician and Austurias (Celtiberans and the seven the Celtic nation) so that we invited new reviews (Ruiz Vieytez, 2003, on the similarities and differences between Irish and Basque, and O'Rourke 2011 on the similarities and differences between Irish and Galician). All the same, mindful that both Scots and Irish were up against a 'large' language and were eager to draw comparisons with other languages 'eclipsed' (as D. Ó Riagáin 2003 puts it) by larger languages. Accordingly, we invited presentations about Estonia (Tender 2011), Tatarstan (Solnishkina 2011) and Ukraine (Pavlenko 2005, 2011), where the local languages were being eclipsed by Russian, Poland where Kashubian was being eclipsed by Polish (Wicherkiewicz 2005), and Belgium, where Walloon was being eclipsed by French (Fauconnier 2003; also Carruthers 2003). Finally, we were eager to hear about countries where multilingualism is the norm: Slovenia (Novak-Lukanovič 2009) and Hungary (Solymosi 2011). In a Preface to the first volume, Cormack (2000) comments briefly on languages in Kosovo. Finally, the acceptance of Irish as an official language of the EU was greatly advantaged by the recognition of Maltese, the subject of another paper (Zammit-Ciantar 2005).

To the symposia also came scholars who had researched the linguistic situation here. Cordula Bilger presented a PhD thesis on 'the language of the Troubles' to the University of Zürich (Bilger 2007), part of which was presented in 2002. Göran Wolf

---

[35] We are grateful to all those who have helped with translation, especially Philip Campbell, Malachy Duffin, and Dónall Mac Giolla Chóill for translations from Irish, Dolina MacLennan and Maolcholaim Scott for translations from Scottish Gaelic, and Máire Uí Bhaoill from French. We are indebted to TOBAR Productions, Tandragee, An Chultúrlann, POBAL and others, and Donegal County Council for the supply and use of translation equipment.

[36] Kirk and Ó Baoill 2002, for instance, has papers in Irish (Muller), Gaelic (Mac Ille Chiar), Scots (Macafee) and Ulster Scots (Parsley) as well as English.

(Technische Universität Dresden), whose paper on Northern Ireland sociolinguistics was presented at the 2007 symposium (Wolf 2011), ran a Hauptseminar in 2008–09 on Northern Ireland Language and Politics, which he will run again in 2011. We know our publications have been used as set texts at the University of Aberdeen and the National University of Ireland, Galway. No doubt, there will be many other uses of which we are unaware.

To make contributions to the symposia came above all scholars of world-class standing: John Edwards (Francis Xavier, NS), Jean-Luc Fauconnier (Brussels), Markku Filppula (Joensuu), Andreas Fischer (Zürich), Manfred Görlach (Köln, twice), François Grin (Geneva, twice), Stephen May (Waikato), Kevin McCafferty (Bergen), Dónall Ó Riagáin (formerly of EBLUL), Robert Phillipson (Copenhagen Business School), Eduardo Ruiz-Vieytez (Bilbao), Tove Skutnabb-Kangas (numerous affiliations), Nancy Stenson (Minnesota), Colin Williams (Cardiff), and Joe Zammit Ciantar (Valetta and Naples).[37]

In addition, we welcomed the following minority language experts: Tomasz Wicherkiewicz (Gdansk), Alexander Pavlenko (Taganrog, Russia, twice), Sonja Novak-Lukanovič (Ljubljana, Slovenia), Bernadette O'Rourke (Galician), Judit Solymosi (Budapest), Tönu Tender (Turku, Estonia), and Marina Solnishkina (Kazan, Tatarstan).

To the rather different eighth symposium in 2008 we welcomed, in addition to numerous world-class UK and Ireland academics, Leith Davis (Simon Fraser, Vancouver), Iain McCalman (Sydney), Katie Trumpener (Yale), and Julia Wright (Dalhousie, Halifax).

As well as the world coming to the symposia, we have been beckoned by the world. During the ten years of the symposia, John Kirk gave invited talks in Berlin, Bonn, Chemnitz, Chisinau, Dresden, Freiburg, Potsdam and Tallinn; Dónall Ó Baoill gave invited talks in Halifax, NS and Vancouver, BC. A related volume of papers arising from a conference on minority languages in Europe held in Dublin, *Voces Diversae* (Ó Riagain 2006), was launched at the Irish Embassy to the EU in Brussels, at which John Kirk gave an address.

We have also been aware that policy issues were not topics to be left to academic researchers alone, but needed input from all sides: government ministers,[38] politicians,[39] civil servants[40] and all their advisers,[41] statutory and institutional practitioners,[42]

---

[37] We also thank Jo Lo Bianco Melbourne for his effort in trying to contribute by video link from Chile in September 2010.

[38] Government Ministers: Seán Farren, MLA 2000, Carmel Hanna, MLA 2002, Éamon Ó Cuív, TD, Mike Russell, MSP 2001 and Mike Watson, MSP 2002. Over the years, many who had been invited were not able to accept; for instance, to the 2010 symposium were invited Nelson McCausland, MLA, Pat Carey, TD, and again Michael Russell, MSP.

[39] Politicians: Ian Adamson, MLA 2005, Alasdair Allan, MSP 2000, Esmond Birnie, MLA 2003, Irene McGugan, MSP 2001, 2002, as a stalwart before election, Ian James Parsley 2000, 2001a, 2001b, 2002, 2005, and the Lord Laird of Artigarvan 2001.

[40] Civil servants: Patricia McAlister 2003, Stephen Peover 2002 and Edward Rooney 2001 from Northern Ireland; Brendán Mac Cormaic 2001, Seán Ó Cofaigh 2001, Bertie Ó hAinmhire 2001, and from the Republic of Ireland; various officials from DCAL and from the Scottish Executive have also attended.

[41] Edmund 2002.

[42] E.g. from Northern Ireland: Mark Adair 2000 and Mari FitzDuff 2000 from the Northern Ireland Community Relations Council, McCoy 2001, 2003, 2011 and Mac Póilin 2011 from ULTACH Trust, Muller 2002, 2011 from POBAL; from the Republic of Ireland: Ó Cearnaigh 2009, Ó Coisdealbha 2011a, 2011b from the Irish Language Commissioner's Office, Ó hAoláin 2009, 20011a, 2011b, 2011c from Údarás na Gaeltachta; Ó Murchú 2000, 2002, 2011 from Comhar ma Múinteoirí Gaeilge; and from Scotland: Campbell 2009 and MacIver 2011 from Bòrd na Gàidhlig, Mackay, R. 2011 from the University of the Highlands and Islands, West and MacLeòid 2009 from Highlands and Islands Enterprise.

linguists,[43] language consultants,[44] language historians,[45] lawyers,[46] educationalists,[47] anthropologists,[48] broadcasters,[49] journalists,[50] media consumers,[51] economists,[52] writers of all kinds,[53] actors, producers,[54] film-makers,[55] librarians,[56] activists,[57] as well as interested and informed individuals.

To the symposia also came broadcasters and media people eager for content and coverage. There was regular annual coverage on BBC Northern Ireland's Irish Language magazine programe *Blas* and on its Ulster-Scots magazine programme *Kist o' Wurds*. In the Republic of Ireland, the symposia have featured on TG4 and Raidió na Gaeltachta. In Scotland, there was coverage at times on the BBC's Gaelic Service, Craoladh nan Gàidheal, Radio nan Gàidheal and BBC Alba (now MG Alba).

A further strength of the symposia grew out of the regular involvement or participation of a core group of individuals, who willingly provided encouragement and advice as the series developed: John Corbett, Andy Eagle, Gavin Falconer, François Grin, Michael Hance, Dauvit Horsbroch, Derrick McClure, MBE, Gordon McCoy, Seosamh Mac Donnacha, Aodán Mac Póilin, Janet Muller, Róise Ní Bhaoill, Pádraig Ó hAoláin, Chris Spurr, Ian James Parsley, and especially to Kenneth MacKinnon, Wilson McLeod, Dónall Ó Riagáin, and John Walsh. We are hugely indebted to those individuals for their unstinting support over the years, and for all their help in making suggestions and guiding us in the right direction. We owe a very considerable amount to Dónall Ó Riagáin for generously making available his considerable expertise in language policy formulation and for introducing us to the many European minority language experts whom we came to invite. And much less would have been achieved without the support of the AHRC RCISS, for which core funding we are indebted to

---

[43] Armstrong 2011, Bilger 2002, Corbett 2002, Corbett and Anderson 2011, Corbett and Douglas 2003, Dolan 2002, Dunbar 2001, 2003, 2009, 2011, Eagle 2001, 2011a, 2011b, Falconer 2001, 2005, 2011, Gupta 2002, Hickey 2009, Kirk, 2000b, 2009, 2011; Kirk and Kallen 2011, Lamb 2005, Loester 2009, Macafee 2001, 2002, MacCaluim 2011, McClure 2002, Mac Ionnrachtaigh 2011, MacKinnon 2001, 2003, 2009, 2011, MacLeod, M. 2011, McLeod 2002, 2003, 2005, 2009a, 2009b, 2011, Millar 2009a, 2009b, 2011, Munro 2011, Ní Dhúda 2011, Ó Duíbhín 2003, Ó Giollagáin 2005, Ó Laighin 2005, Ó Riagáin, P. 2009, Phillipson 2002, Robinson 2011a, 2011b, Skutnabb-Kangas 2002, Smith 2005, Unger 2009, Walsh 2002, 2003, 2009, 2011, Walsh and McLeod 2007, 2011, Wolf 2009.
[44] Ó Riagáin, D. 2000, 2001, 2003, 2009a, 2009b, 2011a, 2011b.
[45] Andrews 2000, Connolly 2009, McCafferty 2009. [46] Hadden 2000.
[47] de Bhál 2002, Douglas 2002, Galloway 2011, Harris 2002, 2011, Mac Ille Chiar 2002, MacDonnacha 2011, MacIver, M. 2002, McKendry 2002, Mac Nia 2002, MacNeil 2011, Malcolm 2011, Munro 2011, Ní Fheargusa 2002, Nig Uidhir 2002, Niven 2002, Ó Baoill 2011, Ó Coinn 2002, Robertson 2002, Rohmer 2002.
[48] McCoy 2001, 2003, 2011.
[49] Caimbeul 2011, Cormack 2003. Cunningham 2003, Eirug 2003, Hegarty 2003, Kay 2011, McHardy 2003, Mac An Iomaire 2003, MacKay 2009, MacLennan 2003, MacNeill 2003, Ní Nuadhain 2003, Ó Ciardha 2003, Ó Cuaig 2003, Spurr 2003.
[50] Blain and Gifford 2003, Cormack 2003, Law, A. 2003, Mac Donald 2003, MacLeod 2009, Ó Pronntaigh 2003.
[51] Ó Clochartaigh 2003, Ó hEadhra 2011, Robinson 2003, Titley 2003.
[52] Bradley 2009, Birnie and King 2003, Chalmers 2003, 2009, Chalmers and Danson 2011, Grin 2003, 2009, Walsh 2003, 2009, Mac Donnacha 2003, MacLeod 2009, McLeod 2003, 2009, Ó Cearnaigh 2009, Williams 2009.
[53] Brown 2009, 2011, Findlay 2003, Herbison 2005, Paisley 2003, Purves 2003, Titley 2005, Whyte 2005.
[54] Grant 2003.
[55] O'Rawe 2003.
[56] Delargy 2001, 2011.
[57] Hance 2005, 2009 and Horsbroch 2000, 2001a, 2001b, 2002 from the Scots Language Centre; Law, J. 2003, 2011 from the Scots Language Society; Smith and Montgomery 2005 from the Ulster-Scots Language Society.

Tom Devine and Cairns Craig, and the Centre's Boards. We are also deeply indebted to our external funders, especially Foras na Gaeilge, Colmcille, and the Ulster-Scots Agency, and we are especially grateful to Deirdre Davitt and Maolcholaim Scott for their personal commitment to our work.

Whereas, for the AHRC RCISS, we became obliged to produce an annual volume, there was also a willingness to subvent these publications. Each volume produced by Cló Ollscoil na Banríona has been funded by Foras na Gaeilge. The Ulster-Scots Agency supported Kirk and Ó Baoill (2000, 2003, 2005). The Northern Ireland Community Relations Council supported Kirk and Ó Baoill (2000, 2001, 2002 and 2005). Colmcille supported Kirk and Ó Baoill (2009, 2011a, and 2011b). To each of these funders we are extremely grateful. We have always been delighted to acknowledge that the Northern Ireland Community Relations Council 'aims to promote a pluralist society characterised by equity, respect for diversity and interdependence.' We also wish to recognise that those funders were willing to support the publication of Irish, Gaelic, and different varieties of Scots in the same volume.

And so evolved the formula for these symposia to provide and provoke critical reflection and discussion in language policy pertaining to the Gaeltacht and Scotstacht.

Publication

As desired by the AHRC RCISS, we have produced an annual publication, thereby ensuring an after-life for the symposia and a more permanent contribution concerning language policy in the three jurisdictions. As already mentioned, we produced multilingual volumes, which, despite general support for linguistic diversity, are quite a rarity. The list of references below also serves as a comprehensive bibliography of the publications generated by the symposia.

We were able to use the volumes in our teaching. John Kirk has used them on his *Language, Culture and Politics* undergraduate module, in which the BSLCP volumes formed the basis for many final assignments, including some on languages other than English. Dónall Ó Baoill uses the texts on his MA course on the *Sociolinguistics of Irish*. We know that the books are set texts at the University of Aberdeen and the National University of Ireland, Galway, and no doubt elsewhere, too.

John Edwards (2006) concludes his review of vols. 1–12 of our *Belfast Studies in Language, Culture and Politics* series, as follows:

> The books reviewed here present a large number of valuable perspectives on current linguistic conditions in the British Isles. Of special significance is the central focus on Northern Ireland, since material dealing with (southern) Irish language, culture, and politics has typically been more available; this focus is a reflection of contemporary trends within Britain, and, in a larger context, within the European Union. Overall, it is hard to think of a more immediate and up-to-date introduction to Scottish and Irish sociolinguistics and the sociology of language than that provided by this fine and expanding set of volumes. And, as with all significant discussions of particular contexts, the coverage here also offers insights whose value extends in much more general directions. On both counts, the series editors, John Kirk and Dónall Ó Baoill, deserve our thanks.

The BSLCP series has attracted other publications, each of which is germane to our concerns, especially Ó Riagáin (2003, 2005). There have been two monographs on Gaelic (Lamb 2008, which, in an appendix, includes an excellent grammar of contemporary Gaelic, reviewed by Ní Laoire 2008; and MacCaluim 2008, reviewed by MacKinnon 2008 and Dorian 2009); a monograph on Irish (Mac Corraidh 2007), a selection of essays on the translation of literary topics in and out of Irish (Dillon and Ní Fhríghil 2008), and a thesis about attitudes to all aspects of language across the Northern Ireland border (Zwickl 2002). Finally, Irish-Scottish studies more broadly feature in four volumes of research papers (Kirk and Ó Baoill 2001, Longley *et al.* 2003, Alexander *et al.* 2004, McClure 2004, and Alcobia-Murphy *et al.* 2005).

Outcomes

As the list above shows, we intentionally and successfully attracted to the symposia a very broad range of participants. For those engaged in the promotion of minority languages, we provided a suitable forum for cross-fertilisation. We encouraged communities to consider and reflect on their heritage in new and refreshed ways. We injected into the debate new information, models, insights, and case-studies. We believe we also helped non-academics to learn and adapt new skills. We encouraged and accommodated the use of the minority languages. Because of the dual-strand approach of symposia and publications, we further believe that we raised awareness and fostered an enhanced understanding of our diverse language heritages in Ireland and Scotland. We have examined the role of Government policies and legislation; we have provided academic leadership through bringing together and bridging the sectors; we have generated critical syntheses and made recommendations; and we have cast some reciprocal illumination on comparable linguistic situations in Europe.

We believe we have had both political and policy outcomes. We injected scientific right-mindedness and rigour into the debates both on Irish and Scots and gave support and confidence to many in the wider community willing to respect the views of academic research and science. In particular, both Ministers and civil servants from the Governments or Executives of each jurisdiction took part and presented papers or gave addresses, most of which were published (see above). We impacted on civil servants, officials, advisers and opinion-formers through our publications that Scots in Northern Ireland is *not* a language separate from Scots in Scotland. To the question about what Scots in Scotland is, we have offered numerous approaches and categorisations. We know that debates on an *Irish Language Act* for Northern Ireland have been influenced by our publications, and that we have influenced public policy, especially on linguistic diversity and multiculturalism in Northern Ireland more generally, even from before the *Belfast Agreement* of 1998.

A clear achievement was the creation of a volume of studies about economic development through language following Grin's four paradigms for doing so: 'the firm, market and management paradigm', 'the development paradigm', 'the language sector and multiplier paradigm', and 'the welfare paradigm'.

A further achievement has been the creation of a specialist network comprising language practitioners, policy-makers, educationalists, and many others, with academics and researchers. Within the network, we have created consultative relationships as well as a sustainable and mutually beneficial set of multi-participative partnerships.

Because we have deliberately targeted both the Gaeltacht and the Scotstacht as well as the pairs of languages within each jurisdiction, we have provided that 'cultural corridor' which has proven necessary for the debate in Northern Ireland between Irish and Ulster Scots (the dubious debate about equality and the need for Part III recognition for Ulster Scots). In so doing, we feel that we have strengthened the language policy sectors within UK and the Republic of Ireland. It was a need which we identified and have filled. At the 2010 symposium, several board members of Bòrd na Gàidhlig were present. During his tenure as CEO of Foras na Gaeilge, Seosamh Mac Donnacha attended every symposium. Members of each of our funders' boards have attended the symposia throughout the series.

We have also benefited the general public through the media attention we have attracted and through our support for policies which promote respect for language and its use.

Thus, we would contend, as a package of symposia and publications, which created a symbiosis for debate and discussion, Language and Politics has made impact. We have made contributions to knowledge, understanding, analysis, policy, planning, skills, and, ultimately, it was argued, to an enhancement in the quality of life. Furthermore, the content of the symposia and volumes suggests to us the verdict of a significant and original contribution to the improvement of Irish-Scottish relationships and the development of Irish and Scottish Studies. We set the bar high at the outset, and we believe we have lived up to these expectations.

Language and Politics has also been financially successful, attracting external investment of up to 2–3 times the initial AHRC RCISS investment, and similar amounts again for publications. In a nutshell, ten years of Language and Politics generated *c*. £250,000. We also believe that the chemistry and synergy between ourselves, linked to our imagination and desire to create something new, our hands-on-ness, and also our initiative and entrepreneurship, have all valuably contributed to its success. For the symposia and publications, we acknowledge with heartfelt gratitude once again the financial assistance which we have received.[58]

At an individual level, Dónall Ó Baoill has been a member of POBAL's research group which in 2009 delivered to the Department of Education a two-year research publication on *The Specialist Educational Needs of Bilingual (Irish/English) Children Attending All-Irish Schools in Northern Ireland*, funded by the Department of Education. Its recommendations will now become part of the Department of Education's future planning initiatives. In November 2000, Ó Baoill was appointed by the Minister for Education in Northern Ireland as one of six trustees of Iontaobhas na Gaelscolaíochta, which co-ordinates the work of the All-Irish Education Trust and provides support for Comhairle na Gaelscolaíochta (Council for All-Irish Medium Education). The function of the Trustee Board has been mainly of a financial nature, with a budget of £2.5 million pounds for the first three years. In 2005, he was appointed for appointed for a second five-year term. Since 2001, Ó Baoill has also acted as an adviser to DCAL's Language Diversity Section on matters relating to Irish Translation and Standardisation problems in Irish.

John Kirk was short-listed in 2003 for the UNESCO Linguapax Prize, which is awarded every year by the UNESCO Linguapax Institute in Barcelona.[59] In 2008, he formed a consortium of academics and language advisers which bid – and was short-listed – for the Scottish Government's Scots Language Audit. Since 2000, Kirk has

---

[58] We also acknowledge funding from the Northern Ireland Community Relations Council for funding towards the publication of several volumes of symposia proceedings.
[59] According to the Linguapax Institute in Barcelona, 'The prizes are awarded to linguists, researchers, professors and members of the civil society in acknowledgement of their outstanding work in the field of linguistic diversity and/or multilingual education ... or in improving the linguistic situation of a community or country.'

been a member of the Scottish Parliament's Cross-Party Group on the Scots Language. He was a founder member of the Forum for Research on the Languages of Scotland and Ulster in 1985 and has been its Treasurer since 2004. He was also a nominee to the Ministerial Advisory Group on Scots.

In all of these ways, we have enhanced the reputation of Queen's University Belfast by acting as a catalyst for debate on language policy.[60]

Whither Now?

After ten symposia and just as many volumes of proceedings, we feel that on Language and Politics we have certainly delivered. With some satisfaction, we could retire gracefully.

However, the business of language policy development is ongoing, with yet more work to be done. There comes to mind immediately the *20-Year Strategy for the Irish Language 2010–2030* in the Republic, the desire for an *Irish Language Act* and an Ulster-Scots Academy in the North, the need for Gaelic Plans on the part of public authorities in Scotland, and the Scottish Government's response to the report of the Ministerial Advisory Group on Scots and ensuant developments – all material enough for another symposium or several more. There will almost certainly be more Government initiatives in the coming years. We have created a network of about a hundred or so individuals active in the field who could readily be called upon for co-operation and support.

A strength of our success, we cannot stress too strongly, has been the availability and generosity of funding. Our role within the AHRC RCISS always ensured our core funding, which we were then able to offer as our contribution for external or matching funding. Without that initial funding, the securing of external funding would almost certainly have proven much more difficult.

However, it may be possible to turn the funding arrangement inside out. As our funders have backed us unflinchingly, there might be a case for those organisations to mount a series of symposia themselves, carrying all the administrative and financial arrangements, but subcontracting the programming and editing of proceedings to ourselves or others. That way, financial management would rest with the funders. We know that Foras na Gaeilge has undertaken a number of projects jointly with the Ulster-Scots Agency.

During the past ten years, there have two other exciting developments at university level: the expansion of Sabhal Mòr Ostaig and the creation of Acadamh na hOllscolaíochta Gaeilge within the National University of Ireland, Galway, which would appear to have very similar functions and objectives. The Mission Statement of Sabhal Mòr Ostaig reads:

> Sabhal Mòr Ostaig is committed to being a centre of excellence for the development and enhancement of the Gaelic language, culture and heritage, by providing quality educational, training and research opportunities through the medium of Scottish Gaelic; and by interacting innovatively with individuals, communities and businesses, to contribute to social, cultural and economic development.

---

[60] At the AILA Conference in Essen in August 2008, it was proposed that Queen's University Belfast might be a possible venue for Inaugural Conference of the International Society for Language Policy and Language Planning Advisers, intended to be a society of professional accreditation.

The Mission Statement of Acadamh na hOllscolaíochta Gaeilge reads:

> The mission of an tAcadamh is to promote and exhibit innovation among the Irish language community, within the Gaeltacht areas and outside those areas. This innovation will enhance the social, cultural, economic and language development of those communities and of people of Ireland in general. To bring this mission to fruition, the objective of an tAcadamh is to promote the sustainable development of university courses, research, services and university activities through the medium of Irish and their delivery and administration.

Both colleges offer a range of graduate and postgraduate degree programmes through the medium of Gaelic and Irish respectively. In so doing, they are promoting the use of Gaelic and Irish both among the college communities as well in the their catchment areas. Each college's activities are greatly enhanced by co-operative links within the wider Gaelic and Irish communities. An tAcadamh offers courses in Business Administration, Communications – Radio and Television Broadcasting, Translation Studies, Interpreting, Language Planning, Education, the Arts and Information Technology.

Sabhal Mòr Ostaig also plays a leading role in the promotion of the Gaelic arts and culture and hosts a programme of residencies for artists in music, literature and the visual arts. Each college provides opportunities and high-quality facilities for in-depth research in these areas, too. An tAcadamh's academic co-ordinator, Seosamh Mac Donnacha, a regular contributor to our symposia (cf. Mac Donnacha 2003, 2011a, 2011b) has a particular interest in pursuing research into organisational and strategic aspects of language planning. Sabhal Mòr Ostaig is home to a number of major creative and cultural research projects such as Tobar an Dualchais,[61] Faclair na Gàidhlig and the multimedia and design company Cànan, and a new £5.29 million partnership project called *Soillse*[62] ('Enlightenment') has been set up to support the Gaelic language and culture.

In his inaugural lecture, 'Theory, Research and Other Dirty Words in Language Policy and Planning', in December 2010, Soillse's Senior Research Professor, Rob Dunbar, argued that theory and research can aid Gaelic revitalisation and explored ways in which the work of specialists can be useful to Gaelic language campaigners.

In a press release at the time of his lecture, Dunbar comments, as follows:

> A common feature of minority language maintenance and revitalisation movements is the fundamental role that passionate activists have in them. Frequently, though, they have only a limited background in language planning theory or practice, and a lack of information to inform and to guide their development initiatives. Although specialists can provide insights and knowledge to these movements, the relationship between specialists and activists can at times be difficult,

---

[61] Its Scots title is *The Kist o Riches*, indicative of its sizeable Scots component. See www.tobarandualchais.co.uk.
[62] *Soillse* is headed by the University of the Highlands and Islands, especially its partner colleges Sabhal Mòr Ostaig on Skye and Lews Castle College on Lewis, and the universities of Aberdeen, Edinburgh and Glasgow. The four institutions are working with key agencies, including the national development agency Bòrd na Gàidhlig, to boost national and local efforts to reverse the decline of the Gaelic language, and to encourage the use of Gaelic in areas where it has not traditionally been spoken.

due to a variety of factors which could be summed up by the phrase 'culture clash'. In my lecture, the theoretical tools relevant to language policy and planning for minority languages such as Gaelic, the experience on which such tools are based, and the research needs and priorities which such tools help us to define, will be considered. Can theory and research inform and support policy-making and practice in ways that allow us to avoid the 'culture clash'?

A major success of our Language and Politics symposia was the bridging of that very relationship between specialists, activists and practitioners.

It strikes us that Acadamh na hOllscolaíochta Gaeilge and Sabhal Mòr Ostaig would form a natural partnership for the purpose of continuing the appraisal of language policy development in these islands. Queen's University Belfast would make an obvious third partner. Whether such a Phase II of Language and Politics concerned itself solely with the Irish-Gaelic continuum or whether the Scots continuum should continue in parallel still needs further discussion.

Within the UK, of course, further partnerships could be added – notably with Welsh and Cornish, and yet remain within the UK's responsibilities under the European Charter. Given its recognition by the European Charter, Manx, too, might be considered.

Any such tie-ups need not exclude the exploration of European partnerships. Our symposia (as well as others such as *Voces Diversae*) have shown the value of such comparisons, and various European models have been applicable to the local situations – e.g. Strubell's Supply and Demand Catherine-Wheel Model for Language Planning (Strubell 1999, quoted in McLeod 2009: 153–4) or Grin's four Language and Economic Development paradigms (Grin 2009). The EU Commission for Education, Culture, Multilingualism and Youth has many funds.[63] Currently, the Union has 23 official languages and over 60 indigenous regional and minority languages – some of which have local official status, such as Sami, Sorbian, Sardinian and Basque.

The website on 'EU Languages and Language Policy' states that 'EU language policies aim to protect linguistic diversity and promote knowledge of languages – for reasons of cultural identity and social integration, but also because multilingual citizens are better placed to take advantage of the educational, professional and economic opportunities created by an integrated Europe. The goal is a Europe where everyone can speak at least two other languages in addition to their own mother tongue.'

Within its programme on Multilingualism, the Commission has issued a number of key policy documents in the last few years. These 'language policy milestones' mark key stages in the formulation of current multilingualism policy.[64] The most recent is the *Strategic Framework for Co-operation on Education and Training* (2009), in which there is a call for further Commission action to promote language learning, e.g. for adults as part of vocational training, and to help migrants learning the language of the host country. In 2008, there appeared the EU *Strategy for Multilingualism* (2008) which sets out what the EU should be doing to promote language learning and protect linguistic diversity. Also in 2008, there appeared *Multilingualism: An Asset for Europe and a Shared Commitment* (2008), which assesses what needs to be done to turn linguistic diversity into an asset for solidarity and prosperity, and an *Inventory of EU Actions in the Field of Multilingualism*, which is a full report on action to promote languages in all fields. In

---

[63] For an overview of funding possibilities, see ec.europa.eu/education/languages/eu-programmes/index_en.htm.
[64] For an overview, see ec.europa.eu/education/languages/eu-language-policy/index_en.htm.

2007, there took place an online consultation on multilingualism, which later made available both the results and the discussion that followed. Finally, in 2005, a *New Framework Strategy for Multilingualism* appeared as the first strategy of its kind but has now been superseded by the 2008 strategy. Thus, there is already in place a considerable amount of European thinking about language planning and language strategies for a Phase II to connect with and build on.

In the EU, 2010 was the target date for many initiatives. New initiatives have since been set for 2020, under a strategic framework for European co-operation in education and training entitled 'Education and Training 2020 – Diverse Systems, Shared Goals'. This framework is intended to build on progress made under the previous Education and Training work programme and has set four strategic objectives: making lifelong learning and mobility a reality; improving the quality and efficiency of education and training; promoting equity, social cohesion and active citizenship; enhancing creativity and innovation, including entrepreneurship, at all levels of education and training. These would certainly lend themselves as objectives for a Phase II project.[65]

A further possibility for future Language and Politics symposia might be more theoretical – to set up a project critical reflection upon the merits and demerits of language policies in a broad range of situations, with a view to establishing afresh the top-down criteria for the components of a first-rate policy. A start may have been made by the EU as well as by recent textbooks which are concerned with policies on a worldwide basis. That, too, might well form a theme for a further symposium or two.

However, there is a final, not inconsiderable point which we have already mentioned and wish to end on. These symposia and publications arose from a voluntary collaboration between a Celticist and a Scotticist who happened to be in the same place at the same time, who found each other eager to push back the boundaries of their respective disciplines, and who found that their different sets of skills and expertise, the interpersonal chemistry of their rather different personalities, and their willingness to be flexible and adaptable, all enabled them to work extraordinarily well together. Such productive inter-disciplinary links are rare, but it would be a not insignificant factor if others were to build on our foundations. As we have repeatedly acknowledged, we Language and Politics was a genuine partnership, which we simply could not have undertaken without each other.

---

[65] ec.europa.eu/education/languages/eu-language-policy/doc120_en.htm.

References

Adair, M. 2000. 'Boundaries, Diversity and Inter-culturalism : The Case of Ulster-Scots'. In eds. Kirk and Ó Baoill, 2000. 143–7.
Adamson, I. 2005. 'The Ullans Academy'. In eds. Kirk and Ó Baoill. 2005. 65–8.
Alcobia-Murphy, S., Archbold, J., Gibney, J. and C. Jones, eds. 2005. *Beyond the Anchoring Grounds: More Cross-currents in Irish and Scottish Studies*. Belfast Studies in Language, Culture and Politics 14. Belfast: Cló Ollscoil na Banríona.
Alexander, N., Murphy S. and A. Oakman, eds. 2004. *To the Other Shore: Cross-Currents in Irish and Scottish Studies*. Belfast Studies in Language, Culture and Politics 12. Belfast: Cló Ollscoil na Banríona.
Allan, A.J. 2000. 'Language and Politics: A Perspective from Scotland'. In eds. Kirk and Ó Baoill. 2000. 127–31.
Andrews, L.S. 2000. 'Northern Nationalists and the Politics of the Irish Language: The Historical Background'. In eds. Kirk and Ó Baoill. 2000. 45–63.
Armstrong, T.C. 'Bilingualism, Restoration and Language Norms'. In eds. Kirk and Ó Baoill. 2011b. 172–9.
Bakker, P. 2006. Review of [Kirk and Ó Baoill 2002b]. *Language in Society* 35: 429–32.
Bilger, C. 2002. 'War Zone Language: Language and the Conflict in Northern Ireland'. In eds. Kirk and Ó Baoill. 2002. 318–26.
Bird, B. 2004. Review of [Kirk and Ó Baoill 2002a]. *Scottish Language* 23: 118–20.
Birnie, E. and S. King. 2003. 'Not such a big deal? The Economy–Language Interaction'. In eds. Kirk and Ó Baoill. 2003. 224–8.
Blain, N. and A. Gifford. 2003. 'Scottish political Identity Construction in the Media; Learning and Teaching Questions around the Theme of Inclusiveness'. In eds. Kirk and Ó Baoill. 2003. 119–30.
Blair, T. 2010. *A Journey*. London: Hutchinson.
Bradley, F. 2009. 'Regional Innovation Environments in the Knowledge Society: Identifying a Place for Irish'. In eds. Kirk and Ó Baoill. 2009. 81–91.
Brown, I. 2009. 'Drama and Literature in Scots as an Economic Generator'. In eds. Kirk and Ó Baoill. 2009. 196–203.
Brown, I. 2011. 'Drama as a Means for Uphaudin Leid Communities'. In eds. Kirk and Ó Baoill. 2011a. 243–8.
Caimbeul, D. and E. Green. 2011. 'Observations on Bilingualism in Digital Media'. In eds. Kirk and Ó Baoill. 2011b. 180–6.
Campbell, A. 2009. 'Making Gaelic Work for Scotland'. In eds. Kirk and Ó Baoill. 2009. 111–6.
Carruthers, J. 2003. 'The Walloon-Scots Comparison: Are There Further Parallels with Other *Langues d'Oïl?*' In eds. Kirk and Ó Baoill. 2003. 303–8.
Chalmers, D. 2003. 'The Economic Impact of Gaelic Arts and Culture: A Response to François Grin'. In eds. Kirk and Ó Baoill. 2003. 245–9.
Chalmers, D. 2009. 'Mapping Language, Arts, Culture and Community: Continuity and Change'. In eds. Kirk and Ó Baoill. 2009. 130–3.
Chalmers, D. and M. Danson. 2011. 'The Economic Impact of Gaelic Arts and Culture in Glasgow'. In eds. Kirk and Ó Baoill. 2011a. 176–87.
Connolly, P. 2009. 'The Divergent Development of the *After*-Perfect in Irish and Scottish Gaelic'. Paper given at Ninth Language and Politics Symposium, Aberdeen.

Corbett, J. 2002. 'The Language Component in the 'Higher-Still' Examinations in 'English': Confessions of an Item-Writer for a Token Exam'. In eds. Kirk and Ó Baoill. 2002. 203–11.

Corbett, J. and W. Anderson. 2011. 'Using it or Losing it? Scots and Younger Speakers'. In eds. Kirk and Ó Baoill. 2011a. 225–37.

Corbett, J. and F. Douglas. 2003. 'Scots in the Public Sphere'. In eds. Kirk and Ó Baoill. 2003. 198–210.

Cormack, M. 2003a. 'Programming for Gaelic Digital Television: Problems and Possibilities'. In eds. Kirk and Ó Baoill. 2003. 83–7.

Cormack, M. 2003b. 'The Case for a Weekly Gaelic Newspaper in Scotland'. In eds. Kirk and Ó Baoill. 2003. 95–9.

Cormack, R.J. 2000. 'Preface: Kosovo in the Spring'. In eds. Kirk and Ó Baoill. 2000. 1–2.

Cunningham, M. 2003. 'BBC Radio Scotland and Scots'. In eds. Kirk and Ó Baoill. 2003. 88–9.

De Bhál, P. 'Teaching through the Target Language: Preparation of Teachers'. In eds. Kirk and Ó Baoill. 2002. 61–4.

Delargy, M. 2001. 'Linguistic Diversity Education Project'. In eds. Kirk and Ó Baoill. 2001. 61–6.

Delargy, M. 2011. 'Buíon dar Slua thar Toinn do Ráinig Chugainn' / 'Some have Come from a Land beyond the Wave'. In eds. Kirk and Ó Baoill. 2011a. 65–8.

Dillon, C. and R. Ní Fhríghil, eds. 2008. *Aistriú Éireann*. Belfast Studies in Language, Culture and Politics 21. Belfast: Cló Ollscoil na Banríona.

Dolan, T.P. 2002. 'Language Policy in the Republic of Ireland'. In eds. Kirk and Ó Baoill. 2002. 144–56.

Dorian, N.C. 2009. Review of [MacCaluim 2007]. *Journal of Sociolinguistics*, 13: 266–9.

Douglas, S. 2002. 'Unblocking the Right Nostril'. In eds. Kirk and Ó Baoill. 2002. 192–7.

Douglas, S. 2003. 'The Scots Leid in the Performing Airts the Day'. In eds. Kirk and Ó Baoill. 2003. 194–7.

Dunbar, R. 2001. 'Minority Language Rights Regimes: an Analytical Framework, Scotland, and Emerging European Norms'. In eds. Kirk and Ó Baoill. 2001. 231–54.

Dunbar, R. 2003. 'Gaelic-medium Broadcasting: Reflections on the Legal framework from a Sociolinguistic Perspective'. In eds. Kirk and Ó Baoill. 2003. 73–82.

Dunbar, R. 2009. 'Two Nations Warring in the Bosom of a Single State? Reflections on the Linguistic (and Cultural) Highland Line'. Paper given at Ninth Language and Politics Symposium, Aberdeen.

Dunbar, R. 2011. 'Bilingualism: Conceptual Difficulties and Practical Challenges'. In eds. Kirk and Ó Baoill. 2011b. 150–62.

Eagle, A. 2001. 'Wha Ye Writin For?' In eds. Kirk and Ó Baoill. 2001. 169–78.

Eagle, A. 2011a. 'German-Speakin Swisserland: A Paitren for Dialect Uphaud'. In eds. Kirk and Ó Baoill. 2011a. 259–65.

Eagle, A. 2011b. 'A Language Strategy for Scots?' In eds. Kirk and Ó Baoill. 2011b. 256–66.

Edmund, J. 2002. 'Ulster-Scots Language and Culture'. In eds. Kirk and Ó Baoill. 2002. 175–82.

Edwards, J. 2006. 'Contemporary Scottish and Irish Studies in Language and Society'. Review Article of *Belfast Studies in Language, Culture and Politics*, vols. 1–12. *Language in Society* 35: 419–27.

Eirug, A. 2003. 'Towards the BBC's Minority Language Policy'. In eds. Kirk and Ó Baoill. 2003. 33–5.
Falconer, G. 2001. 'The Scots Leid in the New Poleitical Institutions'. In eds. Kirk and Ó Baoill. 2001. 135–58.
Falconer, G. 2005. 'Breaking Nature's Social Union: The Autonomy of Scots in Ulster'. In eds. Kirk and Ó Baoill. 2005. 48–59.
Falconer, G. 2007. *Scots: Decline, Revival, Divergence*. Unpublished PhD Thesis, Queen's University Belfast.
Falconer, G. 2011. 'Hiberno-Central as an Unroofed Dialect of Scots'. In eds. Kirk and Ó Baoill. 2011a. 249–58.
Farren, S. 2000. 'Institutional Infrastructure Post-Good Friday Agreement: The New Institutions and Devolved Government'. In eds. Kirk and Ó Baoill. 2000. 121–5.
Fauconnier, J.-L. 2003. 'Les Langues Moins Répandues l'Exemple du Wallon et du Scots'. In eds. Kirk and Ó Baoill. 2003. 294–300.
Findlay, B. 2003. 'Modern Scots Drama and Language Planning: A Context and Caution'. In eds. Kirk and Ó Baoill. 2003. 165–174.
Fischer, A. 2001. 'Language and Politics in Switzerland'. In eds. Kirk and Ó Baoill. 2001. 105–22.
FitzDuff, M. 2000. 'Language and Politics in a Global Perspective'. In eds. Kirk and Ó Baoill. 2000. 75–80.
Foley, N. 2000. 'Language, Discrimination and the Good Friday Agreement: The Case of Ethnic Minority Languages'. In eds. Kirk and Ó Baoill. 2000. 101–5.
Galloway, J. 2011. 'Language Shift and Cultural Change in the Gàidhealtachd: What Prospect for the Cultural Identity?' In eds. Kirk and Ó Baoill. 2011a. 36–43.
Görlach, M. 1985. 'Scots and Low German: The Social History of Two Minority Languages'. In ed. Görlach, M. *Focus on Scotland*. Amsterdam: John Benjamins. 19–36.
Görlach, M. 2000. 'Ulster-Scots: A Language?' In eds. Kirk and Ó Baoill. 2000. 13–31.
Görlach, M. 2001. 'Frisian and Low German: Minority Languages in Hiding'. In eds. Kirk and Ó Baoill. 2001. 67–88.
Grant, D. 2003. 'Language, Culture and Politics: A Theatrical Perspective'. In eds. Kirk and Ó Baoill. 2003. 138–42.
Grin, F. 2003. 'From Antagonism to Convergence: Economics and Linguistic Diversity'. In eds. Kirk and Ó Baoill. 2003. 213–23.
Grin, F. 2009. 'Promoting Language through the Economy: Competing Paradigms'. In eds. Kirk and Ó Baoill. 2009. 1–12.
Gupta, A.F. 2002. 'Privileging Indigeneity'. In eds. Kirk and Ó Baoill. 2002. 290–9.
Hadden, T. 2000. 'Should a Bill of Rights for Northern Ireland Protect Language Rights?. In eds. Kirk and Ó Baoill. 2000. 111–20.
Hance, M. 2005. 'The Development of Scots Language Policy in Scotland since Devolution'. In eds. Kirk and Ó Baoill. 2005. 71–6.
Hance, M. 2009. 'Scots and the Economy'. In eds. Kirk and Ó Baoill. 2009. 183–5.
Hanna, C. 2002. 'Symposium Address'. In eds. Kirk and Ó Baoill. 2002. 20–2.
Harris, J. 2002. 'Research, Innovation and Policy Change: Lessons from the ITÉ Evaluation of the Irish Programme at Primary Level'. In eds. Kirk and Ó Baoill. 2002. 82–99.
Harris, J. 2011. 'Minority Languages, Community and Identity in Ireland and Scotland'. In eds. Kirk and Ó Baoill. 2011a. 11–21.
Hegarty, K. 2003. 'BBC Northern Ireland and Irish'. In eds. Kirk and Ó Baoill. 2003. 36–9.

Herbison, I. 2005. 'The Revival of Scots in Ulster: Why Literary History Matters'. In eds. Kirk and Ó Baoill. 2005. 77–85.

Hickey, R. 2009. 'Linguistic Borders in Ireland'. Paper given at Ninth Language and Politics Symposium, Aberdeen.

Horsbroch, D. 2000. 'Mair as a Sheuch Atween Scotland an Ulster: Twa Policie for the Scots Leid?' In eds. Kirk and Ó Baoill. 2000. 133–41.

Horsbroch, D. 2001a. 'A Twalmonth an a wee Tait Forder'. In eds. Kirk and Ó Baoill. 2001. 123–34.

Horsbroch, D. 2001b. 'A Hairst for a Bit Screive: Writin Historie in Scots'. In eds. Kirk and Ó Baoill. 2001. 187–94.

Horsbroch, D. 2002. 'The Executive o Scotland's Language Apairtheid'. In eds. Kirk and Ó Baoill. 2002. 157–64.

Kaplan, R.B. and R. Baldauf. 1997. *Language Planning: From Practice to Theory*. Clevedon: Multilingual Matters.

Kay. B. 2011. 'Lowsin Time, Yokin Time: The Scots Leid in Twa Thoosan an Seiven'. In eds. Kirk and Ó Baoill. 2011a. 206–11.

Kirk, J.M. 2000a. 'The New Written Scots Dialect in Present-day Northern Ireland'. In ed. Ljung M. *Linguistic Structure and Variation: A Festschrift for Gunnel Melchers*. Stockholm Studies in English XCII. Stockholm: Almqvist and Wiksell International. 121–38.

Kirk, J.M. 2000b. 'Two Ullans Texts'. In eds. Kirk and Ó Baoill. 2000. 33–44.

Kirk, J.M. 2004. 'Archipelagic Glotto-Politics: The Scotstacht'. In ed. Tristram, H.L.C. *The Celtic Englishes III*. Heidelberg: Carl Winter. 339–56.

Kirk, J.M. 2005. 'Language Symbolism and Nation Building: Northern Ireland, Estonia and Moldova'. In ed. Coretchi, A. *From Misunderstanding towards Openness and Collaboration in Multicultural Societies*. Chisinau: Pontos, published for the East-East Program: Partnership Beyond Borders of the Soros Foundation Moldova. 73–100.

Kirk, J.M. 2008. 'Does the UK Have a Language Policy?' *Journal of Irish and Scottish Studies* 1.2: 205–22.

Kirk, J.M. 2009. 'Political Border as Language Border in the North and South of Ireland'. Paper given at Ninth Language and Politics Symposium, Aberdeen.

Kirk, J.M. 2010. 'Devolution and Language'. Paper presented to the Irish-Scottish Forum, The Scottish Parliament, November 2010.

Kirk, J.M. 2011. 'Scotland and Northern Ireland as Scots-speaking Communities'. In eds. Kirk and Ó Baoill. 2011a. 193–205.

Kirk, J.M. and J.L. Kallen. 2011. 'The Cultural Context of ICE-Ireland'. In ed. Hickey, R. *Researching the Languages of Ireland*. Uppsala: Uppsala University Press.

Kirk, J.M. and D.P. Ó Baoill, eds. 2000a. *Language and Politics: Northern Ireland, the Republic of Ireland, and Scotland*. Belfast Studies in Language, Culture and Politics 1. Belfast: Cló Ollscoil na Banríona.

Kirk, J.M. and D.P. Ó Baoill. 2000b. 'Introduction: Language, Politics and English'. In Kirk and Ó Baoill. 2000a. 3–12.

Kirk, J.M. and D.P. Ó Baoill, eds. 2001a. *Language Links: The Languages of Scotland and Ireland*. Belfast Studies in Language, Culture and Politics 2. Belfast: Cló Ollscoil na Banríona.

Kirk, J.M. and D.P. Ó Baoill, eds. 2001b. *Linguistic Politics: Language Policies for Northern Ireland, the Republic of Ireland, and Scotland*. Belfast Studies in Language, Culture and Politics 3. Belfast: Cló Ollscoil na Banríona.

Kirk, J.M. and D.P. Ó Baoill. 2001d. 'Introduction: Language Links'. In Kirk and Ó Baoill. 2001a. xiii–xix.

Kirk, J.M. and D.P. Ó Baoill. 2001d. 'Introduction: Linguistic Politics in the Gaeltacht and Scotstacht'. In Kirk and Ó Baoill. 2001b. 1–21.
Kirk, J.M. and D.P. Ó Baoill, eds. 2002a. *Language Planning and Education: Linguistic Issues in Northern Ireland, the Republic of Ireland, and Scotland*. Belfast Studies in Language, Culture and Politics 6. Belfast: Cló Ollscoil na Banríona.
Kirk, J.M. and D.P. Ó Baoill, eds. 2002b. *Travellers and their Language*. Belfast Studies in Language, Culture and Politics 4. Belfast: Cló Ollscoil na Banríona.
Kirk, J.M. and D.P. Ó Baoill. 2002c. 'Introduction: Language Planning and Education: Linguistic Issues in Northern Ireland, the Republic of Ireland, and Scotland. In Kirk and Ó Baoill. 2002a. 1–19.
Kirk, J.M. and D.P. Ó Baoill. 2002d. 'Introduction: Travellers and their Language. In Kirk and Ó Baoill. 2002b. 1–8.
Kirk, J.M. and D.P. Ó Baoill, eds. 2003a. *Towards Our Goals in Broadcasting, the Press, the Performing Arts and the Economy: Minority Languages in Northern Ireland, the Republic of Ireland, and Scotland*. Belfast Studies in Language, Culture and Politics 10. Belfast: Cló Ollscoil na Banríona.
Kirk, J.M. and D.P. Ó Baoill. 2003b. 'Towards Our Goals in Broadcasting, the Press, the Performing Arts and the Economy: Minority Languages in Northern Ireland, the Republic of Ireland, and Scotland'. In Kirk and Ó Baoill. 2003a. 1–28.
Kirk, J.M. and D.P. Ó Baoill, eds. 2005a. *Legislation, Literature and Sociolinguistics: Northern Ireland, the Republic of Ireland, and Scotland*. Belfast Studies in Language, Culture and Politics 13. Belfast: Cló Ollscoil na Banríona.
Kirk, J.M. and D.P. Ó Baoill. 2005b. 'Introduction: Legislation, Literature and Sociolinguistics: Northern Ireland, the Republic of Ireland, and Scotland'. In Kirk and Ó Baoill. 2005a. 1–15.
Kirk, J.M. and D.P. Ó Baoill, eds. 2009a. *Language and Economic Development: Northern Ireland, the Republic of Ireland, and Scotland*. Belfast Studies in Language, Culture and Politics 19. Belfast: Cló Ollscoil na Banríona.
Kirk, J.M. and D.P. Ó Baoill. 2009b. 'Language and Economic Development: Northern Ireland, the Republic of Ireland, and Scotland'. In Kirk and Ó Baoill. 2009a. xii–xiv.
Kirk, J.M. and D.P. Ó Baoill, eds. 2011a. *Sustaining Minority Language Communities: Northern Ireland, the Republic of Ireland, and Scotland*. Belfast Studies in Language, Culture and Politics 20. Belfast: Cló Ollscoil na Banríona.
Kirk, J.M. and D.P. Ó Baoill, eds. 2011b. *Strategies for Minority Languages: Northern Ireland, the Republic of Ireland, and Scotland*. Belfast Studies in Language, Culture and Politics 22. Belfast: Cló Ollscoil na Banríona.
Kirk, J.M. and D.P. Ó Baoill. 2011c. 'Introduction'. In Kirk and Ó Baoill. 2011a. 1–8.
Kirk, J.M. and D.P. Ó Baoill. 2011d. 'Réamhrá/Introduction: Strategies for Minority Languages'. In Kirk and Ó Baoill. 2011b. 1–10.
Kirk, J.M. and D.P. Ó Baoill. 2011e. 'Ten Years of Language and Politics: Impact and Whither Now?'. In In Kirk and Ó Baoill. 2011b. 267–99.
Kirk, J.M., Brown, M. and A. Noble eds. forthcoming. *The Cultures of Radicalism in Britain and Ireland*. [in the series *Political Poetry and Song in the Age of Revolution*]. London: Pickering and Chatto.
Kirk, J.M., Noble. A. and M. Brown eds. forthcoming. *The Languages of Resistance*. [in the series *Political Poetry and Song in the Age of Revolution*]. London: Pickering and Chatto.
Laird of Artigarvan, J. Lord. 2001. 'Language Policy and Tha Boord o Ulstèr-Scotch'. In eds. Kirk and Ó Baoill. 2001. 37–42.

Lamb, W. 2005. 'The Sociolinguistics of Contemporary Scottish Gaelic'. In eds. Kirk and Ó Baoill. 2005. 126–37.
Lamb, W. 2007. *Scottish Gaelic Speech and Writing: Register Variation in an Endangered Language*. Belfast Studies in Language, Culture and Politics 16. Belfast: Cló Ollscoil na Banríona.
Law, A. 2003. 'Language and the Press in Scotland'. In eds. Kirk and Ó Baoill. 2003. 105–18.
Law, J. 2003. 'Scrievin anent Scots: A Psychopathological Study o a Puckle Scots Journalism'. In eds. Kirk and Ó Baoill. 2003. 131–7.
Law, J. 2011. 'The Scots Commonty'. In eds. Kirk and Ó Baoill. 2011a. 212–7.
Loester, B. 2009. 'Scotland and Bavaria as Linguistic Communities'. Paper given at Ninth Language and Politics Symposium, Aberdeen.
Longley, E., Hughes, E. and D. O'Rawe, eds. 2003. *Ireland (Ulster) Scotland: Concepts, Contexts, Comparisons*. Belfast Studies in Language, Culture and Politics 7. Belfast: Cló Ollscoil na Banríona.
Macafee, C. 2001. 'Scots: Hauf Empty or Hauf Fu?' In eds. Kirk and Ó Baoill. 2001. 159–68.
Macafee, C. 2002. "Auld Plain Scottis' and Pre-emptive Staunardisation o Inglis'. In eds. Kirk and Ó Baoill. 2002. 165–174.
McAlister, P. 2003. 'The Department of Culture, Arts and Leisure's Language Diversity and Broadcasting Policy'. In eds. Kirk and Ó Baoill. 2003. 29–32.
Mac An Iomaire, T. 2003. 'Irish Language Broadcasting', In eds. Kirk and Ó Baoill. 2003. 49–52.
McCafferty, K. 2001. 'Norway: Consensus and Diversity', In eds. Kirk and Ó Baoill. 2001. 89–104.
McCafferty, P. 2009. 'Language Shift on Headstones in the Donegal Gaeltacht, A.D. 1830–2000'. Paper given at Ninth Language and Politics Symposium, Aberdeen.
MacCaluim, A. 2007. *Reversing Language Shift: The Role and Social Identity of Scottish Gaelic Learners*. Belfast Studies in Language, Culture and Politics 17. Belfast: Cló Ollscoil na Banríona.
MacCaluim, A. 2011a. "From Politics to Practice': A' Cruthachadh Plana Gàidhlig do Phàrlamaid na h-Alba'. In eds. Kirk and Ó Baoill. 2011b. 187–91.
MacCaluim, A. 2011b. "From Politics to Practice': A' Cruthachadh Plana Gàidhlig do Phàrlamaid na h-Alba'. In eds. Kirk and Ó Baoill. 2011b. 192–5.
Macaulay, D. 2002. Review of *Belfast Studies in Language, Culture and Politics*, vols. 1–3. *Scottish Language* 21: 73–7.
McClure, J.D. 1988. *Why Scots Matters*. Edinburgh: The Saltire Society.
McClure, J.D. 1995. *Scots and its Literature*. Varieties of English around the World, G14. Amsterdam: John Benjamins.
McClure, J.D. 1997. *Why Scots Matters*. Second Edition. Edinburgh: The Saltire Society.
McClure, J.D. 2002. 'Developing Scots: How Far Have We still To Go?' In eds. Kirk and Ó Baoill. 2003. 186–91.
McClure, J.D. ed. 2004. *Doonsin' Emerauds: New Scrieves anent Scots an Gaelic*. Belfast Studies in Language, Culture and Politics 11. Belfast: Cló Ollscoil na Banríona.
McClure, J.D. 2009. *Why Scots Matters*. Third Edition. Edinburgh: The Saltire Society.
Mac Cormaic, B. 2001. 'An Struchtúr tacaíochta atá le bunú faoi Alt 31 den Acht Oideachais 1998: An Chomhairle um Oideachas Gaeltachta agus lánGhaeilge'. In eds. Kirk and Ó Baoill. 2001. 227–30.
McCoy, G. 2001. 'From Cause to Quango? The Peace Process and the Transformation of the Irish Language Movement'. In eds. Kirk and Ó Baoill. 2001. 205–18.

McCoy, G. 2003. '*Ros na Rún*: Alternative Gaelic Universe'. In eds. Kirk and Ó Baoill. 2003. 155–64.

McCoy, 2011. 'The Culture of Gaelic in Ireland and Scotland: An Saol Gaelach agus An Saoghal Gaidhealach'. In Kirk and Ó Baoill. 2011b. 235–45.

Mac Corraidh, S. 2008. An thóir an dea-chleachtais: *The Quest for Best Practice in Irish-medium Primary Schools in Belfast*. Belfast Studies in Language, Culture and Politics 18. Belfast: Cló Ollscoil na Banríona.

McCullough, B. 2000. 'Language, Discrimination and the Good Friday Agreement: The Case of Sign'. In eds. Kirk and Ó Baoill. 2000. 91–5.

Mac Donald, C. 2003. 'The Symbolic Value of Gàidhlig in the Scottish Sunday Newspapers'. In eds. Kirk and Ó Baoill. 2003. 100–4.

Mac Donnacha, J. 2011. 'The Role of the University in Sustaining Linguistic Minorities: An Irish Case Study'. In eds. Kirk and Ó Baoill. 2011a. 53–64.

Mac Donnacha, S. 2003. 'Is acmhainn luachmhar eacnamaíochta í an Ghaeilge do Phobal na hÉireann ar fad'. In eds. Kirk and Ó Baoill. 2003. 234–7.

Mac Donnacha, S. 2011. 'The Role of Capacity Building in the Implementation of the 20-Year Strategy for the Irish Language'. In eds. Kirk and Ó Baoill. 2011b. 11–20.

McGugan, I. 2001. 'Scots in the Twenty-first Century'. In eds. Kirk and Ó Baoill. 2001. 29–36.

McGugan, I. 2002. 'More Progress for Scots in the Twenty-first Century'. In eds. Kirk and Ó Baoill. 2002. 23–6.

McHardy, S. 2003. 'Broadcasting and Scots'. In eds. Kirk and Ó Baoill. 2003. 90–2.

Mac Ille Chiar, I. 2002. 'Na toir breith gus nach toirear breuth ort: Tuilleadh 's a' choir measaidh ann am Foghlam na h-Alba'. In eds. Kirk and Ó Baoill. 2002. 111–23.

Mac Ionnrachtaigh, F. 2011. 'Ón Bhun Aníos: Resisting and Regenerating through Language in the North of Ireland'. In eds. Kirk and Ó Baoill. 2011a. 132–55.

MacIver, M. 2003. 'Structures for Gaelic-medium Education'. In eds. Kirk and Ó Baoill. 2002. 56–60.

MacIver, M. 2011. 'Sustaining Minority Languages'. In eds. Kirk and Ó Baoill. 2011a. 188–91.

MacKay, J.A. 2009. 'Gaelic-medium Broadcasting and the Economy'. In eds. Kirk and Ó Baoill. 2009. 175–82.

MacKay, R. 2011. 'Gaelic Plans at the University of the Highlands and Islands'. In eds. Kirk and Ó Baoill. 2011b. 196–202.

McKendry, E. 2002. 'Irish and Curriculum Review in Northern Ireland'. In eds. Kirk and Ó Baoill. 2002. 136–45.

MacKinnon, K. 2001. '*Fàs no Bàs* (Prosper or Perish): Prospects of Survival for Scottish Gaelic'. In eds. Kirk and Ó Baoill. 2001. 231–54.

MacKinnon, K. 2003. 'Celtic Languages in the 2001 Census: How Population Censuses Bury Celtic Speakers'. In eds. Kirk and Ó Baoill. 2003. 250–61.

MacKinnon, K. 2008. Review of [MacCaluim 2007]. *Scottish Language* 27: 111–4.

MacKinnon, K. 2009. 'Celtic Languages in a Migration Society: Economy, Population Structure and Language Maintenance'. In eds. Kirk and Ó Baoill. 2009. 166–74.

MacKinnon, K. 2011. 'Growing a new Generation of Gaelic Speakers: An Action Plan in Response to a Ministerial Initiative'. In eds. Kirk and Ó Baoill. 2011b. 210–20.

MacLennan, I. 2003. 'BBC Craoladh nan Gàidheal: Co sinn?' In eds. Kirk and Ó Baoill. 2003. 67–72.

MacLeod, M[arsaili]. 2009. 'Gaelic Language Skills in the Workplace'. In eds. Kirk and Ó Baoill. 2009. 134–52.

MacLeod, M[ichelle]. 2011. 'The Human Factor: Community Language Workers and National Strategies'. In eds. Kirk and Ó Baoill. 2011b. 221–8.

McLeod, W. 2002. 'Alba: Luchd an Aona-Chànanais agus Buaidh na Cairt Eòrpaich'. In eds. Kirk and Ó Baoill. 2002. 284–9.

McLeod, W. 2003. 'Gàidhlig agus an Eaconamidh: Nàdar nan Deasbadan ann an Alba An-Diugh'. In eds. Kirk and Ó Baoill. 2003. 238–44.

McLeod, W. 2005. 'Bile na Gàidhlig: Cothroman is Cunnartan'. In eds. Kirk and Ó Baoill. 2005. 36–45.

McLeod, W. 2009a. 'Expanding the Gaelic Employment Sector: Strategies and Challenges'. In eds. Kirk and Ó Baoill. 2009. 153–65.

McLeod, W. 2009b. 'Language Legislation in Scotland and Ireland: Challenges of Implementation'. Paper given at Ninth Language and Politics Symposium, Aberdeen.

McLeod, W. 2011. 'Gaelic Language Plans and the Issue of Bilingual Logos'. In eds. Kirk and Ó Baoill. 2011b. 203–11.

Mag Lochlainn, P.A. 2000. 'Language, Discrimination and the Good Friday Agreement: The Case of Gays'. In eds. Kirk and Ó Baoill. 2000. 107–10.

MacNeil, C.A. 2003. 'The State of Gaelic Broadcasting in Scotland: Critical Issues and Audience Concerns'. In eds. Kirk and Ó Baoill. 2003. 60–6.

MacNeil, M. and D.P. Ó Baoill. 2011. 'Research Development and the Implementation of Am Bradán Feasa Programme: Early Thinking of the Potential within a Social Issues / Applied Language Work-Stream'. In eds. Kirk and Ó Baoill. 2011a. 29–35.

Mac Nia, S. 'Irish-medium Assessment and Examinations'. In eds. Kirk and Ó Baoill. 2002. 100–10.

Mac Póilin, A. 2011. 'A Lid for Every Pot: The 20-Year Strategy and Northern Ireland'. In eds. Kirk and Ó Baoill. 2011b. 132–49.

Malcolm, I. 2011. 'Young Protestants and Sustaining Irish in the Protestant Community'. In eds. Kirk and Ó Baoill. 2011a. 44–52.

Matras, Y. 2006. Review of [Kirk and Ó Baoill 2002b]. *Romani Studies* 15: 191–200.

Meier, H.H. 1977. 'Scots is Not Alone: The Swiss and Low German Analogues', In eds. Aitken, A.J., McDiarmid, M.P. and D.D. Thomson. *Bards and Makars*. Glasgow: Glasgow University Press. 201–13.

Meyerhoff, M. 2006. *Introducing Sociolinguistics*. London: Routledge.

Mesthrie, R., Swann, J., Deumart, A. and W.L. Leap. 2009. *Introducing Sociolinguistics*. Second Edition. Edinburgh: Edinburgh University Press.

Millar, R. 2006. 'Burying Alive? Unfocussed Governmental Language Policy and Scots'. *Language Policy* 5.1: 53–86.

Millar, R.McC. 2009a. 'Dislocation: Is it Presently Possible to Envisage an Economically-based Language Policy for Scots in Scotland?' In eds. Kirk and Ó Baoill. 2009. 186–95.

Millar, R.McC. 2009b. 'The Politics of Scots and its European Analogues'. Paper given at Ninth Language and Politics Symposium, Aberdeen.

Millar, R.McC. 2011. 'Linguistic Democracy?' In eds. Kirk and Ó Baoill. 2011a. 218–24.

Moriarty, M. 2006. Review of [Kirk and Ó Baoill 2003a]. *Journal of Sociolinguistics* 10: 270–2.

Muller, J. 2003. 'An bhFreastalaíonn Cuid III den Chairt Eorpach ar Réalaíochtaí agus Oideachais Mheán Eile?' In eds. Kirk and Ó Baoill. 2002. 131–5.

Muller, J. 2011a. 'Forbairt Straitéise don Ghaeilge: Cur Chuige Comhbheartaithe á Thógáil'. In eds. Kirk and Ó Baoill. 2011b. 110–18.

Muller, J. 2011b. 'Irish Language Strategy Development: Building a Concerted Approach'. In eds. Kirk and Ó Baoill. 2011b. 119–127.
Munro, G. 2011. 'The *Barail agus Comas Cànain* Survey of Community Language Use, Ability and Attitudes: Some General Observations regarding Future Gaelic Language Policy Planning in Scotland'. In eds. Kirk and Ó Baoill. 2011b. 163–71.
Ní Dhúda, L. 2011a. 'Pobal Gaeltachta an Bhreacbhaile: Cás-staidéar Sochtheangeolaíoch agus Eitneagrafaíoch sa Bheartas Teanga'. In eds. Kirk and Ó Baoill. 2011a. 96–113.
Ní Dhúda, L. 2011b. 'The Breacbhaile Gaeltacht Community: A Sociolinguistic and Ethnographic Case Study in Language Policy'. In eds. Kirk and Ó Baoill. 2011a. 114–31.
Ní Fheargusa, J. 'Struchtúir Éagsúla an Ghaeloideachais'. In eds. Kirk and Ó Baoill. 2002. 52–5.
Ni Laoire, S. 2008. Review of [Lamb 2007]. *Scottish Language* 27: 115–8.
Ní Nuadhain, M. 2003. 'Irish Language Broadcasting'. In eds. Kirk and Ó Baoill. 2003. 53–7.
Nic Craith, M. 2001. 'Concepts, Rights and Languages'. Review of [Kirk and Ó Baoill 2000a]. *The Irish Review* 28: 147–51.
Nig Uidhir, G. 2002. 'Initial Teacher Training for Irish-medium Schools'. In eds. Kirk and Ó Baoill. 2002. 65–75.
Niven, L. 2002. 'Nae Chiels: Scots Language in Scotland'. In eds. Kirk and Ó Baoill. 2002. 198–202.
Novak-Lukanovič, S. 2009. 'Economic Aspects of Language: The Case of Slovenia'. In eds. Kirk and Ó Baoill. 2009. 37–53.
Ó Baoill, D.P. 2001. 'Language Planning and the Sociolinguistics of Register'. In eds. Dickson, D., Duffy, S. Cathakson, D, Ó hÁinle C. and I. Campbell Ross. *Ireland and Scotland: Nation, Region, Identity*. Dublin. 32–8.
Ó Baoill, D.P. 2002. 'Curaclam, Pleanáil, Sochtheangeolaíocht agus Réimeanna Teanga'. In *Curaclam na Gaeilge*. LCCXXX11, Maigh Nuad: An Sagart. 7–18.
Ó Baoill, D.P. 2004. 'The Changing Face of the Irish Language'. Invited plenary lecture presented at the International Conference on the Languages of Ireland, hosted by the Canadian Association for Irish Studies, Halifax, NS.
Ó Baoill, D.P. 2005. 'Language Planning and Implementation in Gaeltacht Areas and the Future of Irish'. Paper presented at Éigse Uladh (International Symposium on Bilingualism and Language Planning).
Ó Baoill, D.P. 2006a. 'Minority Language Revival and Revitalization – Lessons and Pitfalls: The Case of Ireland'. First Guest Lecture as Lansdowne Visiting Professor at the University of Victoria, BC.
Ó Baoill, D.P. 2006b 'Language Standardization and the Role of Dialect'. Second Guest Lecture as Lansdowne Visiting Professor at the University of Victoria, BC.
Ó Baoill, D.P. 2006c 'Language Planning Issues and the Practical Application of Language Policies'. Third Guest Lecture as Lansdowne Visiting Professor at the University of Victoria, BC.
Ó Baoill, D.P. 2011a. 'Cultural, Social, Linguistic and Environmental Issues in Minority Language Development and Maintenance'. In eds. Kirk and Ó Baoill. 2011a. 22–8.
Ó Baoill, D.P. 2011a. 'Straitéis don Ghaeilge i dTuaisceart Éireann'. In eds. Kirk and Ó Baoill. 2011b. 128–9.
Ó Baoill, D.P. 2011b. 'An Irish Language Strategy for Northern Ireland'. In eds. Kirk and Ó Baoill. 2011b. 130–1.

Ó Cearnaigh, S. 2009. 'Forbairt Eacnamúil agus Cúrsaí Teanga in Éirinn: Fíricí agus Fáthanna'. In eds. Kirk and Ó Baoill. 54–60.
Ó Ciardha, P. 2003. 'Celtic Language Broadcasting'. In eds. Kirk and Ó Baoill. 2003. 58–9.
Ó Cofaigh, S. 2001. 'An Ghaeilge: Reachtaíocht'. In eds. Kirk and Ó Baoill. 2001. 219–24.
Ó Coinn, S. 2002. 'Struchtúir na Gaelscolaíochta I dTuaisceart Éireann'. In eds. Kirk and Ó Baoill. 2002. 52–5.
Ó Coisdealbha, C. 2011a. 'Cur i Bhfeidhm / Géilliúlacht: Ceachtanna Foghlamtha ó Iniúchadh Scéimeanna Teanga'. In eds. Kirk and Ó Baoill. 2011b. 34–38.
Ó Coisdealbha, C. 2011b. 'Ensuring Implementation/Compliance: Lessons Learned from Auditing Language Schemes'. In eds. Kirk and Ó Baoill. 2011b. 39–42.
Ó Cuaig, S. 'Súil Eile', In eds. Kirk and Ó Baoill. 2003. 47–8.
Ó Clochartaigh, T. 'Spiorad'. In eds. Kirk and Ó Baoill. 2003. 150–4.
Ó Duibhin. C. 2003. 'A Comment on the Presentation of the Results of the Irish Language Question in the 2001 Census of Northern Ireland'. In eds. Kirk and Ó Baoill. 2003. 262–4.
Ó Giollagáin, C. 2005. 'The Sociolinguistics of Contemporary Irish'. In eds. Kirk and Ó Baoill. 2005. 138–62.
Ó hAinmhire, B. 'Coimisiún na Gaeltachta agus an Gaeltacht'. In eds. Kirk and Ó Baoill. 2001. 225–6.
Ó hAoláin, P. 2009. 'Economic Development through Language: The Gaeltacht Experience'. In eds. Kirk and Ó Baoill. 2009. 61–9.
Ó hAoláin, P. 2011a. 'Sustaining Minority Language Communities: Yin and Yang Juncture for Irish!' In eds. Kirk and Ó Baoill. 2011a. 81–8.
Ó hAoláin, P. 2011b. 'Straitéis 20-Bliain na Gaeilge: Promhadh ár gCreidimh'. In eds. Kirk and Ó Baoill. 2011b. 21–6.
Ó hAoláin, P. 2011c. 'The 20 Year Irish Language Strategy: Testing the Faith of Irish Speakers'. In eds. Kirk and Ó Baoill. 2011b. 27–33.
Ó hEadhra, B. 2011. 'Plans, Plans, Plans'. In eds. Kirk and Ó Baoill. 2011b. 231–4.
Ó Laighin, P.B. 2005. 'Stádas na Gaeilge i Réim Theangacha an Aontais Eorpaigh'. In eds. Kirk and Ó Baoill. 2005. 1–15.
Ó Murchú, H. 2000. 'Language, Discrimination and the Good Friday Agreement: The Case of Irish'. In eds. Kirk and Ó Baoill. 2000. 81–8.
Ó Murchú, H. 2002. 'A Response from Ireland'. In eds. Kirk and Ó Baoill. 2002. 279–83.
Ó Murchú, H. 2011a. 'Léargas ar an gCoibhneas Comhaimseartha idir an Earnáil Dheonach / an tSochaí Shibhialta agus Institiúidí Stáit I bPoblacht na hÉireann'. In eds. Kirk and Ó Baoill. 2011b. 76–89.
Ó Murchú, H. 2011b. 'Some Comments on the Current Forms of Relationship between the Voluntary Sector / Civil Society and Organs of the State in the Republic of Ireland'. In eds. Kirk and Ó Baoill. 2011b. 90–109.
Ó Pronntaigh, C. 2003. '*Lá*: A Daily Newspaper in Irish'. In eds. Kirk and Ó Baoill. 2003. 93–4.
O'Rawe, D. 2003. 'Language and the Irish Cinema Question'. In eds. Kirk and Ó Baoill. 2003. 143–7.
Ó Riagáin, D. 2000. 'Language Rights as Human Rights in Europe and in Northern Ireland'. In eds. Kirk and Ó Baoill. 2000. 65–73.

Ó Riagáin, D. 2001. 'Language Rights / Human Rights in Northern Ireland and the Role of the *European Charter for Regional or Minority Languages*'. In eds. Kirk and Ó Baoill. 2001. 43–54.
Ó Riagáin, D. 2003. 'Walloon and Scots: A Response to Jean-Luc Fauconnier'. In eds. Kirk and Ó Baoill. 2003. 301–2.
Ó Riagáin, D. 2009a. 'An Ghaeilge agus an Saol Eacnamaíoch – Athmhachnamh'. In eds. Kirk and Ó Baoill. 2009. 103–10.
Ó Riagáin, D. 2009b. 'Some Green Shots: A Glance at some Recent Positive Developments for Linguistic Diversity'. Paper given at Ninth Language and Politics Symposium, Aberdeen.
Ó Riagáin, D. 2011a. 'The Concept of Gaeltacht: Time to Revisit?' In eds. Kirk and Ó Baoill. 2011a. 89–95.
Ó Riagáin, D. 2011b. 'Irish: A 20 Year Strategy or Just More Waffle? In eds. Kirk and Ó Baoill. 2011b. 71–75.
Ó Riagáin, D. 2003. *Language and Law in Northern Ireland*. Belfast Studies in Language, Culture and Politics 9. Belfast: Cló Ollscoil na Banríona.
Ó Riagáin, D. 2006. *Voces Diversae: Minority Language Education in Europe*. Belfast Studies in Language, Culture and Politics 15. Belfast: Cló Ollscoil na Banríona.
Ó Riagáin, P. 2009. 'Global and Local in Gaeltacht Areas: Corca Dhuibhne 1960–1986'. In eds. Kirk and Ó Baoill. 2009. 92–102.
Ó Riain, S. [2002]. Review of [Kirk and Ó Baoill 2001b]. www.seanoriain.eu/English.htm
O'Rourke, B. 2011. 'Sustaining Minority Language Communities: The Case of Galician'. In eds. Kirk and Ó Baoill. 2011a. 266–80.
Paisley, J. 2003. '*Whit wey fur no?* Scots and the Scripted Media: Theatre, Radio, TV, Film'. In eds. Kirk and Ó Baoill. 2003. 179–83.
Parsley, I.J. 2000, 'Language, Discrimination and the Good Friday Agreement: The Case of Ulster-Scots'. In eds. Kirk and Ó Baoill. 2000. 89–90.
Parsley, I.J. 2001. 'Ulster-Scots: Politicisation or Survival?' In eds. Kirk and Ó Baoill. 2001. 177–80.
Parsley, I.J. 2002. 'Twa Ulster Scotses: Authentic versus Synthetic'. In eds. Kirk and Ó Baoill. 2003. 183–5.
Parsley, I.J. 2003. 'Wad the Ulster-Scots Tongue Richtlie be Gan Foreairt?'. In eds. Kirk and Ó Baoill. 2003. 211–2.
Parsley, I.J. 2005. 'The Ulster Scots: A New Wey Foreairt'. In eds. Kirk and Ó Baoill. 2005. 69–70.
Pavlenko, A. 2005. 'An Eastern Slavonic Perspective on Scots'. In eds. Kirk and Ó Baoill. 2005. 173–8.
Pavlenko, A. 2011. 'Sustaining Minority Language Communities: The Case of Ukrainian in Southern Russia'. In eds. Kirk and Ó Baoill. 2011a. 300–6.
Peover, S. 2001. 'Encouragement and Facilitation: A New Paradigm for Minority Language Education'. In eds. Kirk and Ó Baoill. 2001. 195–204.
Peover, S. 2002. 'The Current State of Irish-medium Education in Northern Ireland'. In eds. Kirk and Ó Baoill. 2002. 124–30.
Phillipson, R. 2002. 'English for Emerging or Submerging Multiple European Identities?' In eds. Kirk and Ó Baoill. 2002. 267–78.
Purves, D. 2003. 'Scots and Identity'. In eds. Kirk and Ó Baoill. 2003. 175–8.
Ricento, T. 2005. *An Introduction to Language Policy: Theory and Method*. Oxford: Wiley-Blackwell.

Robertson, A.G.B. 2002. 'Teacher Training in Gaelic in Scotland'. In eds. Kirk and Ó Baoill. 2002. 76–81.
Robinson, C. 2003. 'Scots in Soaps'. In eds. Kirk and Ó Baoill. 2003. 184–93.
Robinson, C. 2011a. 'The Role of Dictionaries in Sustaining a Language Community'. In eds. Kirk and Ó Baoill. 2011a. 238–42.
Robinson, C. 2011b. 'The Ministerial Working Group on the Scots Language'. In eds. Kirk and Ó Baoill. 2011b. 247–55.
Rohmer, L. 'Specialist Study of Language within the English Higher Curriculum: Approaches to Practice'. In eds. Kirk and Ó Baoill. 2002. 212–20.
Rooney, E. 2001. 'Language Policy Implementation: A DCAL Civil Servant's Perspective'. In eds. Kirk and Ó Baoill. 2001. 55–60.
Ruiz Vieytez, E.J. 2003. 'Basque and Language Rights'. In eds. Kirk and Ó Baoill. 2003. 265–93.
Russell, M. 2001. 'Language and Politics in Scotland'. In eds. Kirk and Ó Baoill. 2001. 23–8.
Salzmann, Z. 2007. Review of [Kirk and Ó Baoill 2002b]. *Language* 83: 220–1.
Simpson, J.M.Y. 2004. Review of [Kirk and Ó Baoill 2003a]. *Scottish Language* 23: 120–2.
Skutnabb-Kangas, T. 2002. 'Irelands, Scotland, Education and Linguistic Human Rights: Some International Comparisons'. In eds. Kirk and Ó Baoill. 2002. 221–66.
Smith, J. 2005. 'The Sociolinguiustics of Contemporary Scots'. In eds. Kirk and Ó Baoill. 2005. 112–25.
Smyth, A. and M. Montgomery. 2005. 'The Ulster-Scots Academy'. In eds. Kirk and Ó Baoill. 2005. 60–4.
Solnishkina, M. 2011. 'Sustaining Minority Language Communities: The Case of Tatarstan'. In eds. Kirk and Ó Baoill. 2011a. 292–9.
Solymosi, J. 2011. 'Sustaining Minority Language Communities: The Case of Hungary'. In eds. Kirk and Ó Baoill. 2011a. 281–5.
Spolsky, B. 2004. *Language Policy*. Cambridge: Cambridge University Press.
Spolsky, B. 2009. *Language Management*. Cambridge: Cambridge University Press. 2010.
Spurr, C. 2003. 'The BBC Northern Ireland Ulster-Scots Unit'. In eds. Kirk and Ó Baoill. 2003. 40–6.
Strubell, M. 1999. 'Polítiques Lingüístiques i Canvi Sociolingüístic a Europa'. In *Polítiques Lingüístiques a Països Plurilingües*. Barcelona: Departament de Cultura de la Generalitat de Catalunya. 9–26.
Tender, T. 2011. 'Sustaining Minority Language Communities: The Case of Estonian.' In eds. Kirk and Ó Baoill. 2011a. 286–91.
Titley, A. 2003. 'The Coming of the Radio'. In eds. Kirk and Ó Baoill. 2003. 148–9.
Titley, A. 2005. 'Irish Literature and its Expression'. In eds. Kirk and Ó Baoill. 2005 103–11.
Unger, J.W. 2009. 'Economic Discourses of Scots on Bourdieu's 'Linguistic Market'', In eds. Kirk and Ó Baoill. 2009. 204–10.
Vikør, Lars S. 1993. *The Nordic languages. Their Status and Interrelations*. Oslo: Novus Press.
Vikør, Lars S. 2001. *The Nordic languages. Their Status and Interrelations*. Second Edition Oslo: Novus Press.

Walsh, J. 2002. 'Language, Culture and Development: The Gaeltacht Commission 1926 and 2002'. In eds. Kirk and Ó Baoill. 2002. 300–17.

Walsh, J. 2003. 'Teanga, Cultúr agus Forbairt I gCás na hÉireann: i dTreo Cur Chuige Nua'. In eds. Kirk and Ó Baoill. 2003. 229–33.

Walsh, J. 2009. 'Ireland's Socio-economic Development and the Irish Language: Theoretical and Empirical Perspectives'. In eds. Kirk and Ó Baoill. 2009. 70–81.

Walsh, J. 2011a. 'Dátheangachas, Idé-eolaíocht agus an *Straitéis 20-Bliain don Ghaeilge*'. In eds. Kirk and Ó Baoill. 2011b. 43–56.

Walsh, J. 2011b. 'Bilingualism, Ideology and the 20-Year Strategy for Irish'. In eds. Kirk and Ó Baoill. 2011b. 57–70.

Walsh, J. and W. McLeod. 2007. 'An Overcoat Wrapped around an Invisible Man? Language Legislation and Language Revitalisation in Ireland and Scotland'. *Language Policy* 7.1: 21–46.

Walsh, J. and W. McLeod. 2011. 'The Implementation of Language Legislation in Dublin and Glasgow'. In eds. Kirk and Ó Baoill. 2011a. 156–75.

Wardhaugh, R. 2009. *An Introduction to Sociolinguistics*. Sixth Edition. Oxford: Wiley-Blackwell.

Watson, A.M.-W. 2000. 'Language, Discrimination and the Good Friday Agreement: The Case of Chinese'. In eds. Kirk and Ó Baoill. 2000. 97–9.

Watson, M. 2002. 'Towards a Language Policy for Scotland'. In eds. Kirk and Ó Baoill. 2002. 27–42.

Watt, J. and A. MacLeòid. 2009. 'Gaelic and Development in the Highlands and Islands of Scotland'. In eds. Kirk and Ó Baoill. 2009. 117–29.

Whyte, C. 2005. 'MacLean and Modernism: 'Remembered Histories''. In eds. Kirk and Ó Baoill. 2005. 86–102.

Wicherkiewicz, T. 2005. 'Kashubian as a Regional Language'. In eds. Kirk and Ó Baoill. 2005. 163–72.

Williams, G. 2009. 'Language and Economic Development'. In eds. Kirk and Ó Baoill. 2009. 13–36.

Wolf, G. 2011. 'On Some Implications of Sociolinguistic Labels'. In eds. Kirk and Ó Baoill. 2011a. 69–80.

Zammit-Ciantar, J. 2005. 'The Making of the Maltese Language'. In eds. Kirk and Ó Baoill. 2005. 179–94.